The Citizen's Guide to

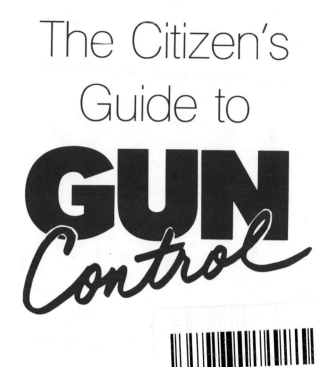

GUN *Control*

The Citizen's Guide to

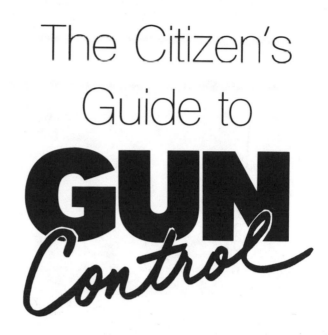

GUN
Control

Franklin E. Zimring

Gordon Hawkins

MACMILLAN PUBLISHING COMPANY
NEW YORK

Collier Macmillan Publishers
LONDON

Macmillan Publishing Company
866 Third Avenue, New York, NY 10022

Collier Macmillan Canada, Inc.

Library of Congress Catalog Card Number: 87-5503

Printed in the United States of America

printing number
3 4 5 6 7 8 9 10

Library of Congress Cataloging in Publication Data

Zimring, Franklin E.
  The citizen's guide to gun control.

  Includes index.
  1. Firearms—Law and legislation—United States.
2. Gun control—United States. I. Hawkins, Gordon,
1919-   . II. Title.
KF3941.Z56 1987   344.73'0533   87-5503
ISBN 0-02-934830-7   347.304533

To Maury Zimring and Hans Zeisel,
proximate causes

Contents

vii

List of Figures

ix

Preface

Americans not only own a greater number and variety of firearms than the citizens of any other modern state, but they also use their guns more often to assault, maim, and kill one another. The United States also has more firearms legislation than any other country in the world. But it is generally acknowledged that the more than 20,000 federal, state, and local gun laws have largely failed to achieve gun control. Firearms continue to multiply, and deaths from guns are at near all-time-high levels.

That situation is the subject, and in part the product, of a debate on gun control that has been going on in America for over half a century. In the 1960s after the assassinations of President John F. Kennedy, Dr. Martin Luther King, Jr., and Senator Robert F. Kennedy, it became a major subject of public passion and controversy. Because gun control is an ideologically dominated and emotionally charged issue, the debate has been heated, acrimonious, and polarized. But it has not been entirely futile and unproductive.

It began in a factual vacuum. Moreover, neither side felt any great need for factual support to buttress foregone conclusions. In the 1960s, there was literally no scholarship on the relationship between guns and violence and the incidence or consequences of interpersonal violence, and no work in progress. More recently, a number of scholars have been provoked into paying sustained attention to the social and policy issues raised by firearms and governmental attempts at their control. There is now a considerable literature available on the relationship between firearms and violence.

On this scholarly level, the debate has not lost its pervasive ideological cast, and much of the literature is still partisan and polemical. But the blithe disregard for factual evidence that characterized earlier confrontations has been replaced by an

xi

emphasis on statistical materials, quantitative methods, and the products of research. Original scholarship on a variety of topics has resulted in increased knowledge, even though many critically important questions have not yet been adequately researched.

Unfortunately, such advances as have been achieved in the scientific study of firearms and violence have had little influence on debate in the larger public arena. There the ancient catchwords, slogans, and rallying cries continue to reverberate with undiminished sonority. A garbled translation of some scholar's research finding may occasionally attract fleeting public attention. But for the most part, what scholars produce is either too technical or too hedged with qualification to make a serviceable political weapon, and it is consequently ignored.

We attempt in this book to bridge the gap by reviewing the familiar focal points of popular discussion and argument on the subject of gun control in the light of the available evidence on the relationship between firearms and violence. It is in part a description of the debate; it is also a contribution to it.

The text is divided into four parts, and each part is subdivided into a number of short textual chapters that are without footnotes but that give sources and references for further reading or bibliographic purposes at the conclusion of the text.

Part One concerns the relationships between firearms and interpersonal violence in the United States. Chapter 1 compares firearms violence in the United States with patterns in other countries and discusses what can be as well as what cannot be inferred from these comparative statistics. Chapter 2 reviews the evidence on the relationship between gun use and the death rate from assault. Chapter 3 discusses the impact of gun use in robbery. Chapter 4 looks at the use of guns—primarily handguns—in defense of households and their occupants. Chapter 5 examines the guns used in crime. And Chapter 6 looks at the relationship between guns and noncriminal violence, suicide, and accidents.

The second part of this book widens the focus from guns and violence to general patterns of gun ownership and use. Chapter 7 critically examines America's historic reputation as a gun culture. Chapter 8 describes current patterns of gun ownership and use in the United States. Chapter 9 discusses whether recent trends in handgun sales constitute a reaction to fear of crime. Chapter 10 examines the relationship between general patterns of ownership and the guns used in crime. Are crime guns really the needle in a haystack that some observers claim? Can we reach the needle without dismantling the haystack? Even then, can reducing the supply of guns to citizens at large have significant impact on the availability of guns for crime? Chapter 11 extends this discussion by analyzing the imposition of restrictions on a citizen's liberty to own guns as creating a special victimless crime, a label that many find significant in their attitude toward criminal prohibitions.

All of this sets the stage for Part Three, a discussion of gun control legislation. Chapter 12 sets out the basic strategies of firearms control—how they are supposed to work and why they might fail. Chapter 13 discusses the pattern of state and local gun laws, and Chapter 14 provides a portrait of existing federal firearms control laws. Chapter 15 reviews the issue of the Second Amendment to the federal Constitution and the scope of the right to bear arms. Chapter 16 collects what little is known about the costs of gun control regimes and the factors that affect those cost.

The final part of this volume concerns the future and the forces that will shape future developent. Chapter 17 discusses the role of ideology in the gun control debate and the costs of excessive ideological zeal. Chapter 18 presents two alternative future roles of the federal government in gun control, and Chapter 19 discusses the social trends that will determine which broad strategy toward civilian handguns will emerge in coming years. Chapter 20 contrasts short-term and long-term effects of regimes of firearms control.

Acknowledgments

The debts we have accumulated in compiling this volume are numerous and spread over two decades. Norval Morris and the late Hans W. Mattick encouraged and supported the program of studies in violence at the University of Chicago Law School, the project that launched Frank Zimring's career in such matters. The Ford Foundation, the National Commission on the Causes and Prevention of Violence, the National Institute of Mental Health, the National Institute of Justice, and the National Science Foundation all supported the research reported in these pages.

The proximate origins of this volume are more recent and specific. Hans Zeisel had long nagged Zimring about the need for a short, nontechnical, and definitive guide to key issues on firearms control. Maury Zimring helped plan the project and drafted large sections of three chapters. The dedication for this book reflects our gratitude.

The staff at the Earl Warren Legal Institute again made it a happy home for our collaborative work. Eric Feldman provided research assistance. Karen Chin word-processed. Cathy Hill paid the bills. Michael Laurence edited. Thanks to all.

We usually circulate our preliminary manuscripts widely. Not this one. John Kaplan of Stanford was our only academic colleague to see this book as work-in-progress. Professor Kaplan's careful review of the manuscript was thus of special value.

Firearms and Violence

1

America's Gun Violence Compared: A Tale of Two Cities

If in the 1970s you had a Detroit friend who was seeking a relatively safe vacation in a setting of near–civil war, the place for him to have visited was Belfast, Northern Ireland; and it still is.

Not that it's dull in Northern Ireland. Between 1969 and 1974 the rate of deaths from violence increased more than twentyfold. In the peak year of 1972 a total of 476 persons were slain; 70 percent of the casualties were civilians. Between January 1969 and June 1974 more than 1,000 people were killed by bombs or shot to death in that small country—a reign of terror sufficient to draw world attention to "bloody Ulster," and to require British military occupation and preventive detention.

But as the FBI reports show, your Detroit friend would have been relatively safe in Northern Ireland at the peak of its troubles, about four times as safe as at home. The city of Detroit (population 1,513,000) had almost exactly the same population as the whole of Northern Ireland (1,536,000) in the early 1970s. Yet in 1973 alone, Detroit police reported 751 deaths from criminal homicide, 24 more than the total number of civilians killed in Ulster during the five and a half years from the beginning of the "troubles" in 1969 through the end of June 1974. In 1973 the rate of civilian deaths in Northern Ireland was about one quarter of that in Detroit. Northern Ireland's troubles continue; however, the death rate there has fallen over the past ten years, while Detroit homicides are higher now than in the early 1970s. Belfast is still much less perilous.

Of course, there are safer places to live than Northern Ireland, but surprisingly few of them are major American cities. During the past twenty years, violent killing in American cities has more than doubled. In 1985 *each* of the ten largest American cities had a homicide rate higher than that experienced at any time in Northern Ireland. We too have our "troubles," but our high rates of criminal violence are such a chronic condition that they are expected and accepted.

In 1967, when Northern Ireland experienced only eight homicides, Detroit had 211; and the average urban homicide rate in the United States was ten times as high as any European city experiencing what it would call a crime wave. The epidemic levels of violence in our city streets are without parallel in any European country.

International Comparisons

The Detroit-Belfast contrast provides an unusually striking example of the kind of comparison that is often cited in the gun control controversy. When gun crime rates in the United States are compared with those in foreign countries, the comparison shows that most industrially developed Western nations experience far lower rates than America. Thus, when the National Commission on the Causes and Prevention of Violence Task Force on Firearms compared the rates of robberies involving firearms and those robberies perpetrated without firearms in England and Wales with comparable rates in the United States, it was found that the U.S. rate of gun homicides was forty times higher than in England and Wales, and the U.S. gun robbery rate was over sixty times higher.

This does not necessarily mean, however, as some proponents of gun control have assumed, that the different rates of gun crimes are caused by differences in gun control, or that adopting foreign firearms control systems in the United States would reduce our firearms violence to the lower foreign levels. Indeed, the rates at which robbery and homicide *with other weapons* are committed in this country are also higher. This and a multitude of other factors—such as traditions and cultural traits—could explain why the rates of firearms crime differ. International comparisons using rates of gun crime can therefore be quite misleading.

More persuasive, however, is the comparison drawn by the National Commission's Task Force on Firearms between the United States and England and Wales which, to control for national differences in the level of violence, related only to the percentages of all robberies and homicides in which guns were used. It was found that, even when the greater incidence of homicide and robbery in the United States was eliminated from the comparison, guns were used in America

---

Table 1-1
FIREARMS HOMICIDES AND ROBBERIES AS PERCENT OF ALL
HOMICIDES AND ROBBERIES, ENGLAND AND WALES VS.
UNITED STATES, 1967

	ENGLAND AND WALES	UNITED STATES
Homicides	18	64
Robberies	6	36

Source: *Firearms and Violence in American Life* (1969), Table 17-2, p. 125.

---

six times as often in robbery and three times as often in homicide as in England and Wales. Moreover, the lower rate of firearms usage in violent crime committed in England and Wales suggests that a firearms control system that makes it substantially more difficult to obtain guns may have something to do with reducing the use of firearms in criminal behavior. The relevant figures are shown in Table 1-1.

Foreign Firearms Laws

Such international comparisons inevitably raise the question whether America's preeminence in regard to firearms violence might not be due to the fact that other countries have more effective firearms control systems, particularly in respect of handgun ownership. This is not to say that systems that appear to work well in other countries with cultures and traditions very different from the United States would necessarily help to lessen the American problem of firearms misuse. At the same time, it would be perverse in any serious consideration of that problem to ignore what other nations have accomplished in dealing with it.

The National Commission's Task Force on Firearms thought it important to examine the variety of ways in which other countries attempt to control the misuse of firearms: Two surveys of foreign firearms laws were made during 1968. The U.S. State Department asked 102 of its diplomatic posts for information on local firearms laws, and the Library of Congress analyzed firearms laws of thirty countries, predominantly in Europe.

These surveys found that the twenty-nine European countries reviewed required either a license to carry a firearm or registration of the ownership or sale of each privately owned firearms, or both. At least five European countries totally prohibited the private possession of handguns. In regard to other types of firearms, the Soviet Union allowed anyone with a hunting license to possess smooth-bore hunting arms. Shotguns were not stringently controlled in England until 1968, when a form of shotgun licensing was established.

In North and South America, fifteen of nineteen canvassed countries reported that they required a license to possess or to carry a firearm or registration of all firearms, or all of these. Paraguay had no controls whatsoever. Mexico had only local controls; El Salvador imposed no restriction except in urban areas; and Nicaragua had no restriction on ownership but did limit the carrying of firearms.

In Asia and Australia, of twenty-one countries canvassed, all required either a license to possess or carry, or registration of firearms, or both. The only exceptions were Australia and New Zealand, which imposed no restriction on shotguns, although they had severe restrictions on handguns; and Afghanistan, which imposed no restrictions on sporting weapons, although it, like Japan, had completely outlawed possession of handguns.

In Africa, twenty-five of the thirty-three nations canvassed required registration of the ownership or sale of firearms. The remaining eight had licensing systems relating to ownership or carrying. Three nations entirely prohibited the possession of handguns, four prohibited possession of military weapons, and one (Algeria) allowed sporting firearms to be possessed only by sporting clubs.

The surveys revealed that foreign countries, with few exceptions, have comprehensive national systems of firearms control. Of course, surveys of this kind based on the texts of firearms laws do not necessarily provide an accurate picture of any country's firearms control system, because they contain no information about enforcement and there may well be substantial gaps between law and practice. Nevertheless, it is notable that those European countries that impose stringent controls on handguns do have relatively low rates of handgun ownership.

Handgun Ownership

The surveys showed that although many foreign countries regulate all firearms without distinguishing between different types, other countries treat handguns and long guns differently, prohibiting or regulating handguns while imposing fewer restrictions on rifles or shotguns. In many countries, the distinction between long guns and handguns was evidently an accepted part of firearms control.

In this connection the National Commission asked the representatives of twenty foreign governments to provide estimates of handgun ownership per 100,000 population. Responses received from ten countries revealed a significant contrast to handgun ownership in the United States. Table 1-2 shows the estimates of handgun ownership for five European countries with significant rural populations—Ireland, Greece, Finland, Yugoslavia, and Austria; two densely populated European countries—the Netherlands and Great Britain; two nations with widespread military training—Switzerland and Israel; and finally Canada and the United States.

Some of the handgun estimates in Table 1-2 deserve special mention. Israel, close to a state of war, still has relatively few private handguns. The Swiss response reflects a distinction between long guns and handguns:

> It is generally felt that the number of handguns in possession of civilians is rather insignificant as there seems to be

Table 1-2
ESTIMATED HANDGUN OWNERSHIP PER 100,000
POPULATION

Ireland	Under 500
Finland	Under 500
Netherlands	Under 500
Greece	Under 500
Great Britain	Under 500
Switzerland	*
Yugoslavia	500–1,000
Israel	1,000
Austria	3,000
Canada	3,000
United States	13,500

*"Insignificant."
Source: *Firearms and Violence in American Life* (1969), Table 16-1, p. 121.

no special need for self protection. On the other hand, every Swiss male of military age keeps his uniform and with it the assault rifle with 48 bullets at home.

Canada, with a frontier tradition and a great expanse of sparsely populated territory, owns handguns at a rate about one-fourth of the U.S. rate.

Of course, the combination of stringent handgun controls and low rates of handgun ownership cannot be taken as evidence of the effectiveness of the controls. Some of the countries might have low handgun ownership even if handgun regulations were not so stringent for the simple reason that their citizens do not care to own handguns. But even in Canada, with a long tradition of firearms use and a permissive licensing system for handguns, the handgun ownership ratio is much lower than that of the United States. It is also relevant to note that although national firearms control may not be as appropriate for the federal system in this country, such large and diverse countries as Canada and Brazil have both adopted national programs of firearms control.

The Home of the Brave

Possibly the most striking feature emerging from international comparisons of firearms ownership and misuse is not the relative absence of controls and the higher levels of violence in the United States but rather the equanimity, if not apathy, with which this situation is accepted in the United States. Why is it, to return to our initial example, that while Detroit has more violence, Belfast, as judged by all measures of expressed social and government concern, has the more serious violence problem?

There is one reason that is specific to the Detroit-Belfast example. It is that the killings in Detroit do not, as in Ulster, where soldiers and police are primarily targets, represent a direct threat to public political order. In Northern Ireland, for example, 300 policemen and soldiers were killed between 1969 and 1974—30 percent of all fatalities. In the United States, while killings of police have increased substantially, they are still about one half of 1 percent of total homicides. To confirm the importance of this element, imagine the distress that would have ensued if fifty policemen had been killed in Detroit last year—and that would be less than 10 percent of the city's homicides!

But there are two other reasons of more general significance. The first is simply that Americans have had ample time to get used to high homicide rates. As Winston Churchill said, "Eels get used to skinning." The relatively benign carnage that produced desperation in Ulster would seem like unprecedented tranquillity to the inhabitants of some of the larger U.S. cities. If we then ask how it is possible to adjust to such rates of urban violence, the answer provides the second reason for America's unique imperturbability.

The principal reason why so many citizens can retain their composure in the face of levels of violence that would topple European governments is that so many of those killed are ghetto dwellers. Most of the urban body count in the United States involves the faceless young black male "noncitizens" who live and die without conspicuous outpourings of social concern.

It is, in fact, misleading to talk of a single homicide rate in American cities, because ghetto-dwelling blacks kill and are killed at rates ten times as high as big-city whites. Urban violence does, of course, affect a broader spectrum of society— small shopkeepers, street robbery victims, and men, women, and children who just happen to be at the wrong place at the wrong time. But the great majority of victims are the black poor.

"No Man Is an Island"

Yet if that is what enables Americans to accept so much violence without alarm and fail to perceive it as a major social problem, not only is our situation precarious but our failure to face up to it is morally indefensible. Both the practical and moral problems involved in dealing with our homicide epidemic by evacuating our cities and accepting violence as an occupational hazard of life for the urban poor are summed up in John Donne's "no man is an island."

The practical problem is that violence is difficult to contain. If we want to protect the small grocer or the local cop from random gunfire, we must also protect the rest of those who so casually become the statistics of urban violence. The same desperate young who kill one another are also frightening the rest of us off the streets. As long as violence is an urban disease, no city dweller is immune from its contagion. And the steps we take to provide real security for ourselves must necessarily help our fellow citizens.

The moral problem lies at the heart of the American dream, for America's greatness has never, throughout the history of the nation, depended on the number, sophistication, and destructiveness of its weapons, whether in military or civilian hands. It has been defined in large measure by what we have done for the dispossessed and the poor—the least advantaged among us.

REFERENCES

Block, Richard, and Franklin E. Zimring. "Homicide in Chicago, 1965–1970," *Journal of Research in Crime and Delinquency* 10 (1973):1–12.

Newton, George D., Jr., and Franklin E. Zimring. *Firearms and Violence in American Life: A Staff Report Submitted to the National Commission on the Causes and Prevention of Violence.* Washington, D.C.: National Commission on the Causes and Prevention of Violence, 1969.

Firearms and Assault: "Guns Don't Kill People, People Kill People"

Ohe of the major arguments against the theory that gun control would save life is that although two-thirds of all homicides are committed with firearms, firearms controls could have no effect on homicide rates because, "human nature being what it is," homicide would continue unabated. Murderers would use the next most convenient weapon. Only the weapons used would change. If guns were eliminated from the scene, more knives, clubs, axes, pieces of pipe, blocks of wood, brass knuckles, or, for that matter, fists would be used. "Guns don't kill people, people kill people."

The classic statement of this argument may be found in Professor Marvin Wolfgang's *Patterns in Criminal Homicide* (1958):

> More than the availability of a shooting weapon is involved in homicide. Pistols and revolvers are not difficult to purchase. . . . The type of weapon used appears to be, in part, the culmination of assault intentions or events and is only superficially related to causality. To measure quantitatively the effect of the presence of firearms on the homicide rate would require knowing the number and type of homicides that would not have occurred had not the offender—or, in some cases, the victim—possessed a gun. . . . It is the contention of this observer that few homicides due to shootings could be avoided merely if a firearm were not immediately present, and that the offender would select some other weapon to achieve the same destructive goal. Probably only in those cases where a felon kills a police officer, or vice versa, would homicide be avoided in the absence of a firearm.

A more recent statement of this position can be found in Wright, Rossi, and Daly's *Under the Gun* (1983):

> Even if we were somehow able to remove all firearms from civilian possession, it is not at all clear that a substantial reduction in interpersonal violence would follow. Certainly, the violence that results from hard-core and predatory criminality would not abate by very much. Even the most ardent proponents of stricter gun laws no longer expect such laws to solve the hard-core crime problem, or even to make much of a dent in it. There is also reason to doubt whether the "soft-core" violence, the so-called crimes of passion, would decline by very much. Stated simply, these crimes occur because some people have come to hate others, and they will continue to occur in one form or another as long as hatred persists . . . if we could solve the problem

of interpersonal hatred, it may not matter very much what we did about guns, and *unless* we solve the problem of interpersonal hatred, it may not matter very much what we do about guns. There are simply too many other objects in the world that can serve the purpose of inflicting harm on another human being . . . although it is true that under current conditions the large majority of gun crimes are committed with handguns (on the order, perhaps, of 70–75% of them), it definitely does *not* follow that, in the complete absence of handguns, crimes now committed with handguns would not be committed! The more plausible expectation is that they would be committed with other weaponry.

The most forcible statements of the opposing viewpoint may be found in the National Commission on the Causes and Prevention of Violence Task Force Report on Firearms and Violence and two Chicago studies of fatal and nonfatal assaults. It is pointed out that although other weapons are involved in homicide, firearms are not only the most deadly instrument of attack but also the most versatile. Firearms make some attacks possible that simply would not occur without firearms. They permit attacks at greater range and from positions of better concealment than other weapons. They also permit attacks by persons physically or psychologically unable to overpower their victim through violent physical contact. It is because of their capacity to kill instantly and from a distance that firearms are virtually the only weapon used in killing police officers.

In addition to providing greater range for the attacker, it is argued, firearms are more deadly than other weapons. The fatality rate of firearms attacks, the Task Force Report noted, was about five times higher than the fatality rate of attacks with knives, the next most dangerous weapon used in homicide. The illustrative data cited are shown in Table 2-1.

The studies also reveal that there was a substantial overlap in the circumstances involved in fatal and nonfatal assaults

Table 2-1
PERCENTAGE OF REPORTED GUN AND KNIFE ATTACKS
RESULTING IN DEATH (CHICAGO, 1965-67)

WEAPONS	DEATH AS PERCENTAGE OF ATTACKS
Knives (16,518 total attacks)	2.4
Guns (6,350 total attacks)	12.2

Source: *Firearms and Violence in American Life* (1969), Table 7-2, p. 41.

with guns and those committed with knives. Four out of five homicides occurred as a result of altercations over such matters as love, money, and domestic problems, and 71 percent involved acquaintances, neighbors, lovers, and family members. In short, the circumstances in which most homicides were committed suggested that they were committed in a moment of rage and were not the result of a single-minded intent to kill. Planned murders involving a single-minded intent, such as gangland killings, were a spectacular but infrequent exception.

Not only did the circumstances of homicide and the relationship of victim and attacker suggest that most homicides did not involve a single-minded determination to kill, but also the choice of a gun did not appear to indicate such intent. The similarity of circumstances in which knives and guns were used suggested that the motive for an attack did not determine the weapon used. Figures obtained from the Chicago Police Department showed the similar circumstances of firearms and knife homicides as shown in Table 2-2.

Further evidence that those who used a gun were no more intent on killing than those who used knives was found in comparing the wound locations and the number of wounds as between those assaults committed with knives and those committed with guns. It was found that a greater percentage of knife attacks than gun attacks resulted in wounds to vital areas of the body—such as the head, neck, chest, abdomen, and back—where wounds were likely to be fatal. Also, many

Table 2-2
CIRCUMSTANCE OF HOMICIDE, BY WEAPON (CHICAGO, 1967)

	GUN (PERCENT)	KNIFE (PERCENT)
Altercations:		
General domestic	21	25
Money	6	7
Liquor	2	8
Sex	1	3
Gambling	2	1
Triangle	5	5
Theft (alleged)	—	—
Children	2	1
Other	41	30
Armed robbery	9	9
Perversion and assault on female	2	7
Gangland	1	—
Other	2	—
Undetermined	6	4
Total	100	100
Number of cases*	265	152

*Another 93 homicides were committed with other weapons.
Source: *Firearms and Violence in American Life* (1969), Table 7-5, p. 43.

more knife attacks than gun attacks resulted in multiple wounds, suggesting that those who used the knife in those attacks had no great desire to spare the victim's life. Nevertheless, even when the comparison was controlled for the number of wounds and the body location of the most serious wound, gun assaults were far more likely to lead to death than knife assaults.

Even so, it might be contended that if gun murderers were deprived of guns they would find a way to kill as often with knives. If this were so, knife attacks in cities where guns were widely used in homicide would be expected to show a low fatality rate, and knife attacks in cities where guns were not so widely used would show a higher fatality rate. But analyses of cities for which the pertinent data were available revealed no such relationship. It appeared that as the number of knife attacks increased in relation to the number of firearms attacks (which presumably happened where guns were less available to assailants), the proportion of knife attacks that were fatal did *not* increase relative to that proportion among gun attacks; if anything, the reverse was the case.

The conclusion that weapon dangerousness independent of any other factors had a substantial impact on the death rate from attack, which has been called the "instrumentality hypothesis," was supported by another study of violent assault in Chicago, which compared low-caliber with high-caliber firearms attacks. This study found that attacks with large-caliber firearms were far more likely to cause death than attacks by small-caliber guns that resulted in the same number of wounds to the same parts of the body.

The authors of *Under the Gun,* cited above, have disputed the conclusions drawn from the evidence presented in the Chicago studies. They dismiss the circumstantial evidence such as the motives of homicide and the frequent involvement of alcohol in killings as inconclusive on whether attacks that cause death are often ambiguously motivated. The similar demographic profiles of fatal and nonfatal attacks are not regarded as evidence that the two groups "are similar in any respect relevant to hypotheses about underlying motivations." The same conclusion apparently was applied to the similarities between victim groups.

The authors never address the possibility that chance elements determine a subsample of fatalities from the universe of those assaulted. The crucial fact that most gun killings, like most nonfatal assaults, involve only one wound is rejected as evidence against a single-minded intent to kill in favor of the conclusion that what distinguishes the hundreds of one-shot killings from thousands of one-shot nonfatal woundings in the same body location by the same sort of people is "a level of marksmanship that one would probably not expect under conditions of outrage and duress." This conclusion is reached without any evidence from the extensive literature on criminal violence.

Indeed, the only evidence offered in support of this hypothesis is drawn from the experience of one of the authors in preparing deer carcasses for home freezers. The relevance of this experience to shooting people in a homicidal situation is explained as follows:

> He is yet to encounter, over a sample of some 15–20 taken deer, even a single deer that was taken with one and only one shot . . . [this] suggests that capable marksmen, armed with highly accurate and efficient weaponry, aiming unambiguously to kill roughly man-sized targets, are seldom able to kill their prey with a single shot. That a much higher proportion of murderers, armed with much less impressive weaponry, kill with a single shot might therefore cause us to wonder just how ambiguous the underlying motives are.

The authors do not consider the possibility that some of the marksmen, even if armed with less accurate and efficient weaponry, might not do better if they could maneuver a few of their deer into the living room. Nor do they consider the alternative hypothesis that many killers are randomly drawn from the larger pool of one-shot assaulters, or discuss why "determined" killers will often stop after one wounding when most guns have a multiple wounding capacity.

It is also curious that the sharp differences in death rates for large-caliber versus small-caliber guns assaults are not considered to be evidence that the objective dangerousness of a weapon has a significant influence on the death rate from assault. The authors briefly examine this data, and they caution that this pattern could also be explained if more determined killers chose larger-caliber guns. The evidence from the weapon caliber study that the pattern holds true even when the attacker probably did not choose the weapon is ignored.

Conclusion

The issue of instrumentality effects from guns in deadly assaults is important in its own right. It is also an instructive example of the practical and philosophical differences between the ideological forces in conflict about gun control. This dispute about instrumentality effects is not so much about the nature of the evidence available but about what that evidence means and how great the burden of proof should be.

The parable of the butchered deer carcass mentioned above seems the closest Wright and his colleagues can come to a personal background in research on criminal violence. Instead of grounding their discussion in a coherent vision of violent assault, they put forward rival hypotheses to each strand of circumstantial evidence individually, conclude that none is strict proof of instrumentality effects by itself, and assume that the cumulative impact of multiple strands of evidence is no more persuasive than any of the individual strands.

When the time came to recommend future research, the authors were prisoners of their own standards. In their report to the federal government, no further investigation of these critical issues was proposed. In their book, the authors leave the impression that nothing is known on the question of what difference guns make and nothing can be done to increase knowledge. The tone, and the level of denial, remind one of the Tobacco Institute's valiant struggle against premature conclusions on the relationship between cigarettes and lung cancer.

It should also be said that the assertion that "unless we solve the problem of interpersonal hatred it may not matter very much what we do about guns" is a nice example of the "root causes" fallacy. The essence of this argument is that if crime control measures are to be effective, they must deal with the "root causes" of crime—in this case "interpersonal hatred." Even the most effective regime of gun control would not totally eliminate homicide and on this argument could be criticized for not having dealt with the "root cause" of the problem.

REFERENCES

Newton, George D., Jr., and Franklin E. Zimring. *Firearms and Violence in American Life: A Staff Report Submitted to the National Commission on the Causes and Prevention of Violence.* Washington, D.C.: National Commission on the Causes and Prevention of Violence, 1969.

Wolfgang, Marvin. *Patterns in Criminal Homicide.* Philadelphia: University of Pennsylvania Press, 1958.

Wright, James D., Peter H. Rossi, and Kathleen Daly. *Under the Gun: Weapons, Crime, and Violence in America.* New York: Aldine, 1983.

Zimring, Franklin E. "Is Gun Control Likely to Reduce Violent Killings?" *University of Chicago Law Review* 35 (1968):721–737.

——— . "The Medium Is the Message: Firearms Caliber as a Determinant of the Death Rate from Assault," *Journal of Legal Studies* 1 (1972):97–123.

3

Firearms and Robbery: Your Money or Your Life

Robbery, the taking of property by force or threat of force, is a major problem in its own right and a central issue in the analysis of violent crime in America. Unlike theft and burglary, robbery is a property crime that frequently threatens the physical security of its victim. Robbery is a crime of violence that strikes many more victims than rape and reaches across boundaries of social distance far more often than aggravated assault. Robbery is the stranger-to-stranger crime that most frequently results in victim death and injury in the United States. It is also the stranger-to-stranger crime most closely associated with guns and the demand for gun control.

The relationship between guns, particularly handguns, and robbery involves a number of complicated issues as well as some simple ones. A preliminary distinction has to be drawn between the relationship between gun use and robbery rates, on the one hand, and the relationship between gun use and robbery outcomes, on the other.

There are some kinds of robbery that are difficult to accomplish without a gun. In those directed at commercial and other well-protected establishments, a handgun is often necessary. Thus, in Chicago, Zimring and Zuehl found that two-thirds of all commercial robberies involved guns, and about nine out of ten of the guns used were handguns. Other types, such as strong-arm robberies of more vulnerable victims or of individuals by groups, can be carried out without guns or any other deadly weapon. Thus, street robberies in Chicago involved guns in 39 percent of all cases. The availability of handguns will clearly influence the rate of robbery directed at targets where guns are necessary, but it may or may not influence the overall robbery rate.

Statistics on the range of injuries from robberies involving guns appear almost benign because the rate of minor injuries from handgun robberies is substantially lower than the rate in other kinds of robbery. In Chicago, for example, only 15 percent of all robbery that led to reported injury involved guns, compared to 43 percent of all robberies. This low rate is because the handgun presents such a potent and credible threat of injury or death. Victims are more apt to comply without actual force being used. Muggers, by contrast, may use force to make the threat of force credible or to obtain the property. But rates of serious injury from handgun robbers are as great as those for other types of robbery.

The death rate from gun robberies is at least three times

Table 3-1
PERCENTAGE DISTRIBUTION OF ROBBERIES AND ROBBERY
KILLINGS BY LOCATION AND WEAPON

	COMMERCIAL ROBBERIES		STREET ROBBERIES		OTHER ROBBERIES	
	KILL-INGS	NON-LETHAL	KILL-INGS	NON-LETHAL	KILL-INGS	NON-LETHAL
Gun	81	67	67	39	83	43
Knife	13	11	11	15	13	15
Other weapon	6	6	17	8	—	8
Personal force	—	17	6	39	4	34
Total	100	100	100	100	100	100
N	16	36	18	150	24	109

Note: Totals may not equal 100 due to rounding.
Source. Zimring and Zuohl. "Victim Injury and Death in Urban Robbery: A Chicago Study." *Journal of Legal Studies* 15 (1986):1, 16

as high as the death rate from knife robberies and greatly exceeds that for strong-arm robberies, as shown in Table 3-1.

By far the most lethal combination in urban robbery is an assailant with a loaded gun and a victim with the will to resist, for loss of life in robbery is strongly associated with active victim resistance. In Chicago it was found that active noncooperation with an armed robber is associated with a death risk approximately fourteen times as great as in robberies with cooperation or passive noncooperation. The resisted robber in commercial cases—stores and shops—is forty-nine times as likely to kill his victim as the robber who meets no resistance from his commercial victim. When the choice is between your money or your life, discretion is evidently the better part of valor. Resistance to robbery with lethal weapons rarely makes sense.

Table 3-2 illustrates the relationship between resistance and robbery death by showing the pattern of resistance for robberies and robbery killings for a one-year period in Chicago (October 1, 1982, to September 30, 1983). The robbery event

Table 3-2
PERCENTAGE DISTRIBUTION OF ROBBERY AND ROBBERY
KILLINGS BY RESISTANCE

	ROBBERY KILLINGS	ROBBERIES
No resistance	34	82
Passive noncooperation	11	10
Active noncooperation	55	8
N	65	348

Source: Zimring and Zuehl. "Victim Injury and Death in Urban Robbery: A Chicago Study." *Journal of Legal Studies* 15 (1986):1, 18

was classified in one of three categories: no resistance noted, passive noncooperation (the victim usually says he or she has no money), and active noncooperation (including refusal, flight, and physical force). It is clear that loss of life in robbery is strongly associated with active victim resistance. Only 8 percent of the robbery cases came under this classification, as compared with 55 percent of the death cases.

The role of resistance in making robbery more dangerous is confirmed by the sharp contrast that exists between gender and the death rate from robbery in Chicago. Female victims of street robbers are killed at one-sixth the rate of male victims, and female victims of commercial robbery are killed less than one-eighth as often as male victims.

Why is it that one in 100 robberies results in the death of the victim? One thing is clear: Even though the robber and his victim are strangers at the outset, a robbery demand under the threat of a deadly weapon initiates a conflict involving a contest of wills if the victim refuses to cooperate. Such conflicts when loaded guns are present are likely to have lethal consequences.

Thus, while the gun is not a necessary element to the crime of robbery, guns make many forms of robbery against defended targets feasible and are a major explanation of robbery killings in the United States. This is of particular importance because robbery is the stranger-to-stranger crime responsible for about 75 percent of felony killings in the United States.

REFERENCES

McDowell, David. "Gun Availability and Robbery Rates: A Panel Study of Large U.S. Cities, 1974–1978," *Law and Policy* 8 (1986):135–148.

Zimring, Franklin E. "Determinants of the Death Rate from Robbery: A Detroit Time Study," *Journal of Legal Studies* 6 (1977):317–332.

Zimring, Franklin E., and James Zuehl. "Victim Injury and Death in Urban Robbery: A Chicago Study," *Journal of Legal Studies* 15 (1986).1–40.

4

Guns for Self-Defense: The Armed Citizen

One of the principal focal points of the gun control debate relates to the ownership and use of guns for self-protection, particularly in urban areas. There are good reasons for this. The guns that are owned for self-defense in cities are mainly handguns. At the same time, the handgun is the criminal's primary firearm, and handguns have become the pivotal issue in the current debate about gun control.

Prior to the National Commission on the Causes and Pre-

29

vention of Violence of 1968, no proposals for a policy of national handgun scarcity had been made since the 1930s. In the years after the commission's report, focus of the handgun debate has shifted almost entirely to restrictive licensing, handgun "bans," and other strategies to prohibit law-abiding citizens from acquiring handguns except under special circumstances. The commission's rejection of middle-of-the-road proposals of the sort endorsed by earlier national commissions sharpened the debate at the same time that it intensified opposition to handgun control among anticontrol groups.

This opposition is understandable when the most common reason for owning a handgun is for household self-defense against home-invading robbers or burglars. Some years ago, a national sample of people with some shooting experience was asked what were good reasons for owning guns. Seventy-one percent of the shooters mentioned self-defense as a good reason for owning a handgun—far more than gave one other good reason. Only 16 percent gave hunting as a good reason for owning a handgun. The responses showing the "good reasons" given for owning different types of firearms are shown in Figure 4-1.

Another poll found that 66 percent of householders with any guns listed "protection" as one reason for having them. More recently, a survey of all U.S. adults found the 71 percent of those owning a handgun said that they owned it only for protection or self-defense.

Those who support restrictive handgun policies argue that self-defense handguns are a very poor investment and that the protection they provide is illusory. Even though the great majority of handguns are kept for household self-defense, it is absolutely clear that the handgun in your house is more likely to kill you or a member of your family than to save your life. In Detroit, Michigan, for example, more people died in one year from handgun accidents than were killed by home-invading robbers or burglars in four and a half years. And it

Figure 4-1 "Good Reasons" for Owning Long Guns and Handguns (United States, 1964)

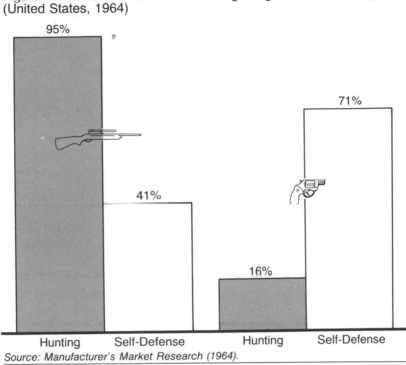

Hunting	Self-Defense	Hunting	Self-Defense

Source: Manufacturer's Market Research (1964).

is rare indeed that a household handgun actually stops the burglar who tries to elude the homeowner, or the home robber who counts on surprise and a weapon of his own. So the gun that will not save your life, more than 99 times out of 100, will not save your color television either.

It would be foolish to think that millions of American families keep handguns merely because they have not read the statistics or to suppose that sending them a copy of the latest gun control article will change their minds. The risk of accidental or homicidal death from a gun in one's home— though far greater than the chances that the gun will save life—is nevertheless small. In the great majority of gun-owning homes, the only real use of the gun is to make its owner feel less uneasy about the possibility that a hostile stranger will invade his home.

This feeling of well-being, although a statistical illusion, is an emotional reality. People will resist the statistics that show otherwise because, if their guns do not give them any real measure of protection, they have no other way to deal with their fears. In addition, everything that makes the handgun a special problem in America also makes it hard to understand that the handgun is not effective against the home-invading criminal. How can something so deadly be so ineffective? Trying to persuade someone that the gun in his house is not really protecting him is like trying to persuade a nervous friend that flying in a jet plane—seven miles above the ground at 600 miles an hour—is really safer than driving the family car to Florida.

Those who oppose handgun controls argue that the ineffectiveness of private weapons as crime deterrents has not been *directly* established. It is *possible* that the widespread ownership of guns keeps the rates of crime and violence below what they would otherwise be. Moreover, a feeling of well-being and belief in safety is in itself a benefit that should not be lightly dismissed. If people feel safer because they own a gun and live more happily because they feel more secure, then their gun ownership has made a substantial contribution to their quality of life.

Another argument that is advanced in favor of the deterrent effect of private firearms involves the suggestion that although the possibility of a home robber or home burglar burglarizing an occupied residence is very small, it is higher than the possibility of his being apprehended and imprisoned. As there is evidence which suggests that the possibility of imprisonment deters at least some robbery and burglary, it is argued that at least some potential robbers and burglars are deterred by the fear of being shot by their intended victims.

It is also argued that the most important deterrent effect of private weaponry is likely to be the *generalized* deterrence that results from the high overall possession rate of firearms among U.S. households. In other words, there may be large numbers of *potential* criminals who do not commit crimes because they know that many citizens are armed and they fear the possibility of getting shot. It is argued that the crime rates might be still higher were it not for firearms, and that the widespread ownership of guns keeps crime and violence below the level it might otherwise reach.

There is no evidence to support this hypothesis, and its proponents acknowledge that this effect could never be detected even in the largest and most sophisticated research effort. It is therefore possible to examine critically only the more specific assertions made by those who claim that private firearms are an effective crime deterrent and means of self-defense.

In the first place, although some crimes are thwarted or foiled by the victim shooting at the offender, the risk to the offender is very small indeed. For example, the Violence Commission Task Force on Firearms reported that in Detroit over the period 1964–1968, at the most no more than two in 1,000 burglaries were foiled by shooting the burglar. Similarly, only about 2 percent at most of all robberies result in the firearms injury or death of the robber. Moreover, the risk to the homeowner's life from burglars is very small.

The situation may be different in regard to business robberies and burglaries. Of all crimes against businesses, robbery is the primary threat to life. In Detroit in five years, fifty persons were killed during robberies of businesses (and six died in business burglaries). The evidence suggests that "protective" firearms might be reducing robbery rates of commercial establishments in high crime areas. Moreover, the *known* possession of firearms may well deter robbers when businesses of a particular kind—such as bars—are known to have firearms for protection. It is not known whether, when, or how much guns protect businessmen, but the possession of firearms by businessmen appears to entail less risk of accident, homicide, and suicide than firearms in the home.

Thus guns may be of some utility in defending businesses, whereas they are very rarely an effective means of protecting the home against either the burglar or the robber. Moreover, this largely illusory defense is purchased at the high price of increased accidents and homicides, and more widespread illegal use of guns.

The argument made by Wright, Rossi, and Daly to the effect that there are at least as many if not more crimes "thwarted" by the victim actually shooting at the offender than there are offenders who are apprehended and imprisoned for their offense is simply mistaken. The argument begins with the assertion that "the burglary of an unoccupied residence, the most common type of home burglary, is clearly not deterrable by any firearms kept in the home, since there is no one home to use them." But this fact, it is said, has no bearing "on whether private weapons are useful deterrents to crimes that occur in a situation or area where they would be potentially deterrable, which is the more important empirical issue."

The argument then runs as follows: 90 percent of all home burglaries occur when no one is at home. If two in 1,000 of all burglaries are foiled by the victim's use of a firearm and 900 in 1,000 occur with no one home, then the actual prevention rate for burglaries committed with a person in the home is roughly 2 percent. This seems a relatively low risk, but it exceeds the risk to a burglar of being apprehended, charged, prosecuted, convicted, and sentenced for the crime. For in 1976 "the overall risk of a burglar being arrested and convicted was only about 1–8% for any given burglary. If half . . . received a prison sentence then the risk of imprisonment was 0.9%."

This conclusion, however, is a statistical illusion. The *overall* risk to the burglar of being foiled is not 2 percent but two in 1,000, even in the optimistic best-case guess by Newton and Zimring, the origin of this figure. The overall risk of imprisonment is nine in 1,000. In other words, the risk of imprisonment is four and a half times the prevention-by-shooting estimate cited. And the burglary "thwarted" under this measure by a gun need not incapacitate the burglar at all, whereas prison for those who serve time may prevent further crimes.

The preventive effects of gun ownership and use on household crime are not measurable and probably small. It almost never pays to confront an armed criminal, because the extra risk to the victim's life is more important than the chance of saving property.

Yet, the need to see guns as effective is based on the feeling of helplessness that citizens encounter because of the threat of household crime. Even though putting burglars in prison is much more important than homeowners using guns, the low rates for catching and convicting burglars are the reason why people grasp at guns and other ephemeral solutions. Greater confidence in law enforcement would doubtless remove the emotive foundation for self-defense guns, and no statistics on cost and benefit will provide emotional comfort without that confidence.

With all the controversy over the costs and benefits of guns for household self-defense, there is one aspect of the matter—on which experts are in unanimous agreement—that has not achieved the recognition we think it deserves: Almost all authorities from gun-control advocates to the National Rifle Association counsel that the loaded gun easily accessible in the bedroom dresser is an invitation to disaster. The risks, from children playing or showing off, from adults who are drunk or frightened or both, or from burglars themselves, are just too great.

The unanimous advice of experts is to store guns in the house in a locked area that is separate from where ammunition for the gun is kept. This warning from manufacturers and gun owner groups should play a far more prominent role in dialogue about guns and self-defense than has been the case in recent years.

REFERENCES

Newton, George D., Jr., and Franklin E. Zimring. *Firearms and Violence in American Life: A Staff Report Submitted to the National Commission on the Causes and Prevention of Violence*. Washington, D.C.: National Commission on the Causes and Prevention of Violence, 1969.

Wright, James D., Peter H. Rossi, and Kathleen Daly. *Under the Gun: Weapons, Crime, and Violence in America*. New York: Aldine, 1983.

5

The Guns
Used in
Crime

O ur discussion in this chapter concerns two questions:
First, what kind of guns are most at risk of being used in violent
crime? Second, how are these guns acquired by those who
misuse them?

37

Crime Guns

With regard to the first question, there is overwhelming evidence that, although only about one quarter of all firearms in the United States are handguns, they are the predominant firearm used in crime. In 1984 firearms were used in the United States in 59 percent of homicides, 36 percent of robberies, and 21 percent of aggravated assaults. In each category the predominance of the handgun is striking. Not only is it the dominant firearm used in homicide nationwide, it is also almost invariably the weapon used when firearms are involved in aggravated assault and robbery, as Figure 5-1 illustrates.

Some corroboration of this can be found in studies that have analyzed information obtained from the distribution of firearms confiscated by the police. Each study confirms the predominance of handguns as being in the region of 77 percent

Figure 5-1 Handguns and Long Guns in Crimes involving Firearms (United States, 1967)

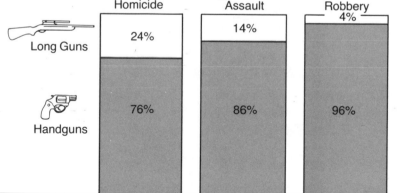

Source: *Firearms and Violence in American Life* (1969), Table 8-1, p. 49.
* 1967 Uniform Crime Report
** Police departments in 10 large cities

to 82 percent. Those studies have also provided another significant piece of information in relation to criminal gun use.

One of the most significant findings from the first mass tracing of handguns seized by the police was that a disproportionate number had been first sold to a retail customer in the relatively recent past. What has been called the "new guns" hypothesis was the product of gun-tracing efforts initiated by the Federal Bureau of Alcohol, Tobacco, and Firearms in 1973. The findings of this tracing of guns seized by the police in New York City are shown in Figure 5-2.

Figure 5-2 Handguns Confiscated in New York City during December 1973 by Year of Original Sale

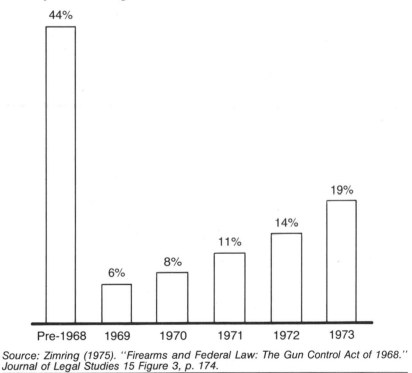

Source: Zimring (1975). "Firearms and Federal Law: The Gun Control Act of 1968." Journal of Legal Studies 15 Figure 3, p. 174.

There were problems associated with drawing general inferences from the New York study. The first was the possibility that police and federal agency sampling procedures had produced a nonrepresentative sample of guns from New York. The second problem was the unusual position of New York as a city in a state that encourages restrictive licensing of handguns, which in that respect is far from typical of other metropolitan areas. Third, the sample reported was from only one city during only one time period. The need for replication seemed obvious.

Subsequently, an attempt to replicate the New York City

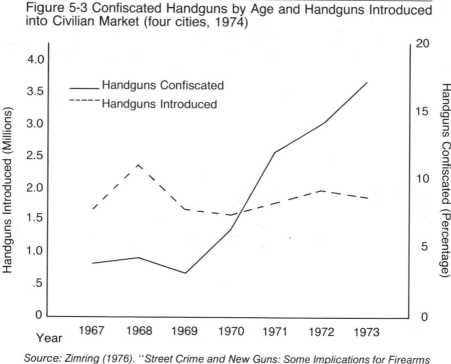

Figure 5-3 Confiscated Handguns by Age and Handguns Introduced into Civilian Market (four cities, 1974)

Source: Zimring (1976). "Street Crime and New Guns: Some Implications for Firearms Control." Journal of Criminal Justice 4, Figure 2, p. 100.

study in a number of other cities with different state and local handgun strategies tended to confirm the "new guns" hypothesis. The new data provided by federal tracing efforts provided information on the age of confiscated handguns in eight cities located in major regional areas in the United States (Dallas, Denver, Kansas City, Oakland, Miami, Minneapolis/ St. Paul, Philadelphia, and Seattle), and revealed a picture of striking intercity consistency. In each city newer handguns dominated the confiscation statistics, and in seven of the eight cities guns produced after 1970 accounted for about half of total traced confiscations.

It might be thought that annual introduction rates of new guns would provide an explanation of the high proportion of new guns among those confiscated. But those rates over the previous decade had been relatively stable (at extremely high levels), and the striking "new gun" effect cannot be explained by noted variation in production and imports. Figure 5-3 shows that this "new gun" phenomenon is not importantly related to differences in recent levels of supply of handguns by comparing annual handgun production and imports with the aggregate confiscation figures for four of the cities.

How Are They Acquired?

Firearms are durable goods. Firearms manufacturers say that they can be expected to last indefinitely if given proper care. It is also to be expected, therefore, that the secondhand market in firearms should be almost as important as the new market. In fact, almost half of all rifles and shotguns and slightly more than half of all handguns are acquired used by their owners. A Harris poll conducted for the National Commission on the Causes and Prevention of Violence found this to be the case, as indicated in Figure 5-4.

New firearms are normally sold by manufacturers and importers to wholesalers, who sell to dealers, who in turn sell

Figure 5-4 How Firearms were Acquired (United States, 1968)

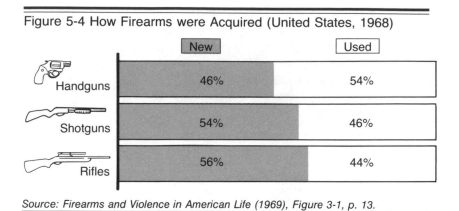

Source: *Firearms and Violence in American Life (1969), Figure 3-1, p. 13.*

to consumers. Wholesalers vary widely in the products they distribute and the territories they cover. Some operate in many states, but most sell primarily in a handful of states surrounding their location and have only a few customers in other states.

The largest share of the more than 150,000 federal firearms licenses are issued to retail dealers ranging from gunshops and sporting goods stores to hardware stores, department stores, and pawnshops. Most of the remaining federal firearms licenses are held by private individuals, who pay the fee to allow them to buy firearms at wholesale prices and transport firearms through the mails.

The Harris poll revealed that whereas new firearms and a large number of used firearms are purchased from sporting goods stores, hardware stores, and other firearms dealers, over half of all secondhand guns are obtained from a friend or another private party. The market for secondhand firearms is shown in Figure 5-5.

The acquisition patterns of firearms used in crime are rather different, although sales of secondhand firearms are apparently a major source of crime guns. With well over 100 million firearms in private hands distributed among half of

Figure 5-5 Sources of used firearms (United States, 1968)

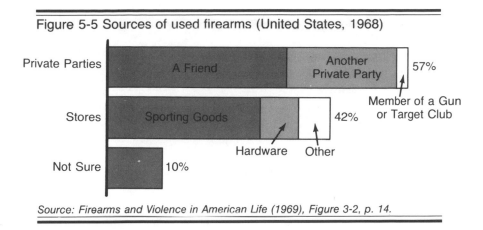

Source: *Firearms and Violence in American Life (1969), Figure 3-2, p. 14.*

the households in the United States, the firearms used in crime are of course only a small fraction of the total. For the criminal, however, the ready availability of guns is a significant advantage.

Although relatively little is known in detail about the firearms used in crime, an attempt was made by the National Commission on the Causes and Prevention of Violence Task Force on Firearms to determine how guns used in crime were acquired. To this end, samples of handguns confiscated in crimes in Detroit and Los Angeles were studied. Both cities require an application to purchase a handgun, but in both cities relatively few of these applications are denied and thus possession of firearms is not significantly restricted.

In Detroit a sample of 113 handguns confiscated by police during shootings in that city during 1968 showed that only 25 percent of the confiscated weapons had been recorded previously in connection with a gun permit application. In Los Angeles a sample of fifty handguns involved in homicides, 100 handguns involved in aggravated assaults, and 100 handguns involved in robberies was analyzed at the request of the task force. Figure 5-6 shows the proportion of firearms for which there was a record of an application. Three-fourths of

Figure 5-6 Handguns Used in Crime: Recorded-Unrecorded (Los Angeles, 1968)

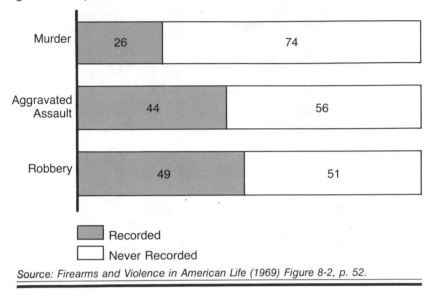

Source: *Firearms and Violence in American Life (1969) Figure 8-2, p. 52.*

the handguns used in homicide and about one-half of the handguns used in the other two crimes had been recorded at some time.

An examination of a subsample of twenty of the confiscated handguns that were once registered, in each category of crime in Los Angeles, compared the name of the last recorded owner with the name of the suspect in the crime committed with the handgun. In crimes in which the handguns used were recorded, the suspect was the last recorded owner in 35 percent of the homicides, 50 percent of the aggravated assaults, and 20 percent of the robberies. In addition, in 5 percent of the homicides and 15 percent of the robberies, the handguns were recorded under the same family name as that of the suspect, suggesting that when a gun is in the household another member of the family may misuse it. But most of the recorded guns used in crime (60 percent for homicide, 50 percent for aggravated assault, and 65 percent for robbery) were apparently used by persons other than the last recorded owners. Since only 6 percent of these weapons had been reported as stolen, sales of secondhand firearms seem to be a major source of firearms used in crime. But guns are almost certainly stolen at a rate higher than the 6-percent figure suggests. Many thefts may go unreported because the owner has never recorded his ownership or does not know the weapon's make or serial number. Figure 5-7 shows the results of the investigation of the subsample.

A recently published study by Wright and Rossi of guns used by state prison inmates shows even greater emphasis on the hand-to-hand market. Only about one in six handguns was acquired through ordinary retail stores while the prisoners report stealing one-third of their handguns and purchasing many of the rest from private parties. As many as two-thirds

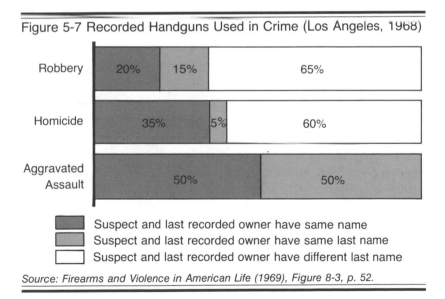

Figure 5-7 Recorded Handguns Used in Crime (Los Angeles, 1968)

Robbery	20%	15%	65%
Homicide	35%	5%	60%
Aggravated Assault	50%		50%

■ Suspect and last recorded owner have same name
▨ Suspect and last recorded owner have same last name
☐ Suspect and last recorded owner have different last name

Source: Firearms and Violence in American Life (1969), Figure 8-3, p. 52.

Figure 5-8 Number of New Handgun Permits Issued in Detroit, (1965–68)

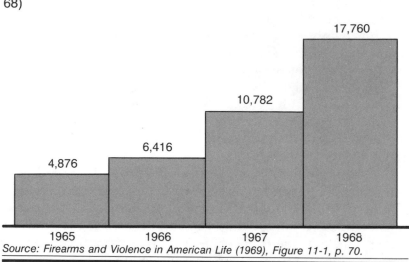

Source: Firearms and Violence in American Life (1969), Figure 11-1, p. 70.

of handguns reported in this study could have been stolen at least once.

The acquisition of guns is in part controlled by availability and accessibility. It might be expected, therefore, that there would be some relationship between general firearms possession and firearms violence. The National Commission on the Causes and Prevention of Violence was established at a time when the country was experiencing a substantial increase both in violent crime and in sales of firearms. The Task Force on Firearms therefore decided to investigate the relationship of gun ownership and gun use in violence.

The investigation was carried out in three different ways. First, a case study was made of a city that had experienced a substantial arms buildup. Second, a comparison was made of gun ownership and gun use in crime in different regions of the country. Third, a study of armed crime in eight major American cities was conducted to determine whether there was evidence that the use of guns in violent crime was related to total gun ownership.

The city selected for study was Detroit. It was found that the increase in handgun sales over the years 1965 to 1968 had been accompanied by parallel increases in violent attacks with firearms, robberies with firearms, and firearms homicides. Because Michigan law requires anyone who wants to buy a handgun to apply for a permit from the local police, the general trend of lawful handgun acquisitions can be determined from the number of permits issued. Figure 5-8 shows the annual rate of handgun permits issued in Detroit from 1965 through 1968. It can be seen that new permits for handguns rose

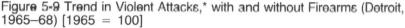

Figure 5-9 Trend in Violent Attacks,* with and without Firearms (Detroit, 1965–68) [1965 = 100]

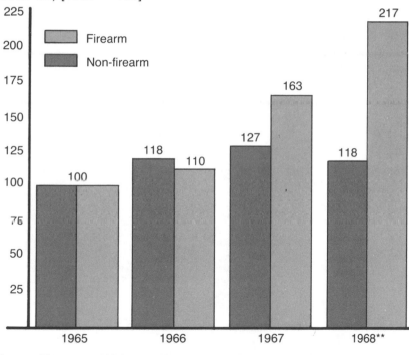

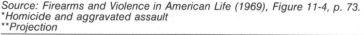

Source: *Firearms and Violence in American Life (1969), Figure 11-4, p. 73.*
*Homicide and aggravated assault
**Projection

sharply during each of the four years, reaching in 1968 a level almost four times that in 1965.

Figures 5-9 and 5-10 show the trends in the use of firearms in violent attacks (homicides and nonfatal aggravated assaults) known to the police in Detroit and also the trend in the use of firearms in robberies from 1965 through 1968. Because the proportion of crimes involving firearms varies with the type of crime, both figures use 1965 as a base year to show the later increases as a percentage of the 1965 level. The figures show that during this period, while attacks not involving firearms rose somewhat, firearms attacks nearly doubled; and that fire-

Figure 5-10 Trend in Robberies, with and without Firearms (Detroit, 1965–68)

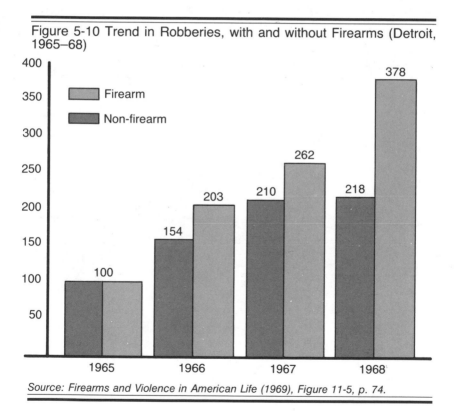

Source: *Firearms and Violence in American Life (1969), Figure 11-5, p. 74.*

arms robberies increased about twice as fast as robberies committed without firearms.

Figure 5-11 shows the homicide trend over the same years. Homicides committed with weapons other than firearms increased by 30 percent over the four-year period, while homicides with firearms increased by 400 percent. In 1965 only 39 percent of homicides involved firearms; by 1968 about 72 percent involved firearms.

The relationship between firearms possession and firearms violence was next examined by comparing different regions of the United States. Figure 5-12 shows the frequency of reported gun ownership in the four basic regions of the country and the percentage of homicides and aggravated assaults in those regions that were committed with firearms. The per

Figure 5-11 Trend in Criminal Homicides, with and without Firearms (Detroit, 1965–68)

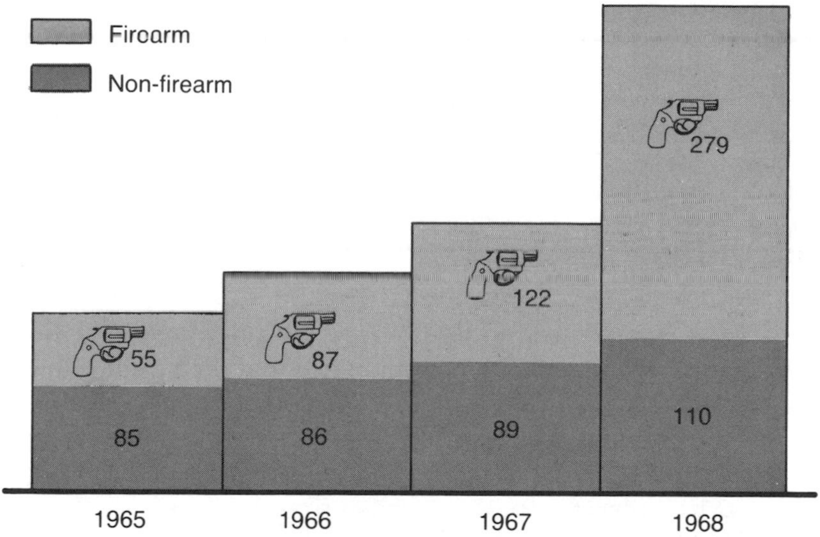

Firearm

Non-firearm

1965	1966	1967	1968
55	87	122	279
85	86	89	110

Source: *Firearms and Violence in American Life (1969), Figure 11-6, p. 74.*

Figure 5-12 Gun Ownership and Percentage Gun Use in Homicide and Aggravated Assault by Region

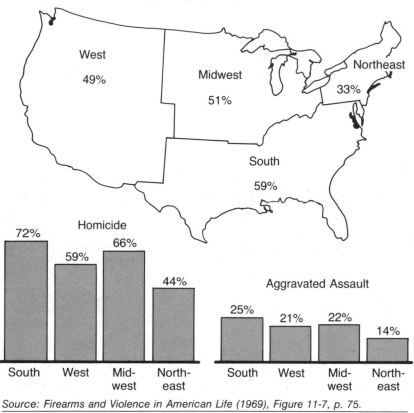

Source: Firearms and Violence in American Life (1969), Figure 11-7, p. 75.

centage of homicides and aggravated assaults involving firearms paralleled firearms ownership, except in the South, which lagged behind the West and Midwest in reported handgun ownership, although it led in total reported gun ownership. The Northeast, with the lowest firearms ownership, also showed the lowest rate of firearms crime.

Finally, an intercity comparison provided further evidence that the use of guns in violent crime is related to the extent of gun ownership. Cities with a high percentage of gun use in one type of violent crime tend to have a high percentage of gun use in other types of violent crime and that cities with low gun use in one crime tend to have low gun use in other crimes. It was further found that the cities with high rates of

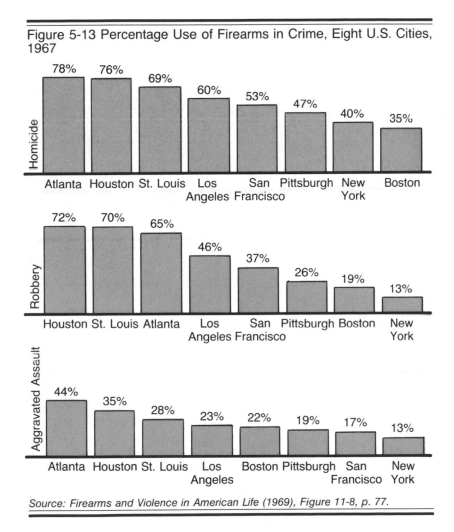

Figure 5-13 Percentage Use of Firearms in Crime, Eight U.S. Cities, 1967

Source: *Firearms and Violence in American Life (1969), Figure 11-8, p. 77.*

gun use in crime were in the South and West, the areas with the highest gun ownership rates. Cities located in areas with relatively low rates of gun ownership, such as New York and Boston, tended to have the lowest rates of gun use in crime. It appeared that the use of guns in violent crime rose or fell in relation to gun ownership. Figure 5-13 shows the results of the comparison.

The relationship between rates of gun introduction and crimes with guns has received some recent attention, although not nearly as much as the importance of the topic would merit. One analysis, made by Professor Gary Kleck, sought to test the hypothesis that new guns have a disproportionate impact on rates of gun violence by comparing trends in gun introduction for the United States as a whole with the same year's homicide and robbery totals. He found no significant relation between gun sales in that year and movements in crime rates during that year.

Two problems with that study deserve mention. The first concerns the absence of a time lag and is correctable. This study, in effect, measured what influence December's gun sales had on last January's gun homicides. The solution to this problem is to "lag," to compare how this year's gun sales relate to next year's movements in gun crime. This is easy to accomplish, but has not yet been done.

The second problem is harder to deal with. The number of guns sold in any particular year is an incomplete and variable measure of trends in handgun availability. For example, the 2.4 million handguns that were introduced in the United States in 1968 probably had a much greater impact on handgun availability and crime than the 2.4 million handguns introduced in the United States in 1975. If the average handgun lasts six years, the 2.4 million handguns coming to market in 1968 replaced perhaps 600,000 handguns that had been introduced about six years before. About three-fourths of all the new guns did not replace old guns, and the impact on gun availability was substantial. But if the over 2 million handguns introduced in 1975 were replacing about the same number of weapons introduced six or seven years earlier, the impact on gun availability, and thus on gun crime, would be more modest.

We do not know the useful life of handguns in the United States, and this hampers our efforts to use sales data to measure trends in gun availability. We do know that the 1960s, with dramatic growth in handgun sales, appear to be a better laboratory for studying the impact of increasing gun availability than later years.

Conclusion

Our conclusion can be simply stated. In the first place, there is overwhelming evidence that the handgun is the principal weapon of criminal misuse. Second, periods of increase in handgun acquisition appear to be associated with increases in firearms violence. Third, samples of handguns confiscated in a variety of urban areas implicate newer handguns as a disproportionate contributor to the offenses that lead to gun confiscation. Fourth, there appear to be significant links between general handgun availability and the use of handguns in violent crimes.

REFERENCES

Kleck, Gary. "The Relationship Between Gun Ownership Levels and Rates of Violence in the United States," in Don B. Kates, Jr., ed., *Firearms and Violence: Issues of Public Policy.* Cambridge, Mass.: Ballinger, 1984.

Newton, George D., Jr., and Franklin E. Zimring. *Firearms and Violence in American Life: A Staff Report Submitted to the National Commission on the Causes and Prevention of Violence.* Washington, D.C.: National Commission on the Causes and Prevention of Violence, 1969.

Wright, James D., and Peter H. Rossi, *Armed and Considered Dangerous: A Survey of Felons and Their Firearms.* New York: Aldine, 1986.

Zimring, Franklin E. "Firearms and Federal Law: The Gun Control Act of 1968," Journal of Legal Studies 4 (1975)133–198; reprinted in Library of Congress, *Improving the Criminal Justice System in the United States*, 94th Congress, 2nd Session, Document No. 94–171.

————. "Street Crime and New Guns: Some Implications for Firearms Control," *Journal of Criminal Justice* 4 (1976):95–107.

6

Accidents, Suicide, and Guns

We deal in this chapter with two noncriminal aspects of firearms violence that may be of crucial importance in making decisions about different gun control regimes. They are important topics and yet have been grossly neglected. The number and determinants of gun accident injuries and deaths has been the subject of only one scholarly study in the almost two decades since the National Violence Commission report: a time-series analysis of Cuyahoga County, Ohio (metropolitan Cleveland), published in the *American Journal of Epidemiology*.

Unfortunately, no sustained attention has been paid to changes in reported firearm accident rates in the vital statistics or in the proportion of handgun accident deaths to total gun accident deaths over time. Changes between urban and non-urban areas in the distribution of gun accidents have gone unstudied. There has been no further research on the relationship between firearms availability and suicide rates.

Firearms Accidents

Gun accidents are significant for three reasons. First, they involve paradoxical costs, that is, costs that for the most part are imposed on precisely those individuals and members of

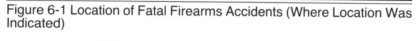

Figure 6-1 Location of Fatal Firearms Accidents (Where Location Was Indicated)

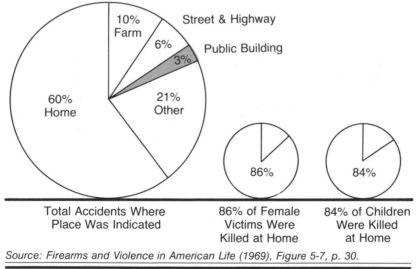

| Total Accidents Where Place Was Indicated | 86% of Female Victims Were Killed at Home | 84% of Children Were Killed at Home |

Source: Firearms and Violence in American Life (1969), Figure 5-7, p. 30.

households the firearms are intended to protect or benefit. The National Commission on Causes and Prevention of Violence Task Force on Firearms reported that 60 percent of accidental firearms deaths occur in the home, and that for women and children the percentages were 86 percent and 84 percent, respectively, as shown in Figure 6-1.

Second, gun accidents involve direct costs that can be easily assessed without raising any problems about human motivation or the possibility that if firearms had not been available some other method might have been employed to achieve the same end. In the case of suicide, other methods— hanging, carbon monoxide, poisonous substances, jumping, and so forth—are almost equally effective possible alternatives. In the case of homicide the next most popular and dangerous weapon, the knife, might in many cases be substituted and

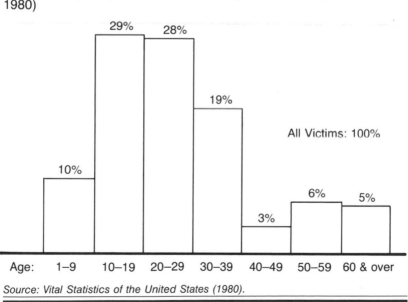

Figure 6-2 Age of Victims of Fatal Handgun Accidents (United States, 1980)

Source: Vital Statistics of the United States (1980).

kill. But in the case of firearms accidents, what has been called the instrumentality problem does not arise.

Finally, firearms accidents provide a classic example of aggregate statistics concealing sharply different patterns in such things as the age and gender distribution of victims, the regional distribution of accidental deaths, and the type of weapon involved. Figure 6-2 shows in greater detail the distribution by age of fatal handgun accident victims. Ten percent are children under ten, and the largest group of handgun accident victims are children between ten and nineteen years of age.

Figure 6-3 shows the rate of accidental deaths from firearms by region of the country. The fluctuation of rates from region to region parallels the pattern of firearms ownership, reflecting the fact that more gun accidents occur where there are more firearms.

Figure 6-3 Accidental Civilian Firearms Deaths by Region (United States, 1966) [annual rate per 100,000]

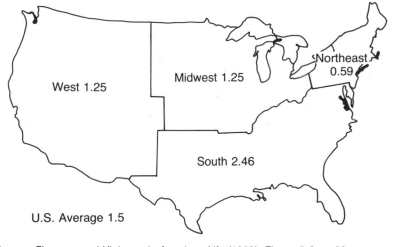

Northeast 0.59

Midwest 1.25

West 1.25

South 2.46

U.S. Average 1.5

Source: Firearms and Violence in American Life (1969), Figure 5-6, p. 29.

Figure 6-4 sets out the information relating to the types of firearms involved in the activities leading to fatal accidents. Although many firearms accidents occur during shooting activities or while cleaning weapons after such activities, others arise from activities that have little to do with proper firearms use. Handgun accidents are more likely to fall into the latter category of accidents, which are *not* related to the shooting sports.

The trend in handgun accidents and gun accidents in the home and in urban areas was significantly up in the 1960s. The time series analysis carried out in metropolitan Cleveland revealed a threefold increase in accidental firearms fatalities in the period 1967–1973, and concluded that a major factor in the rise in those fatalities was the increase in the availability

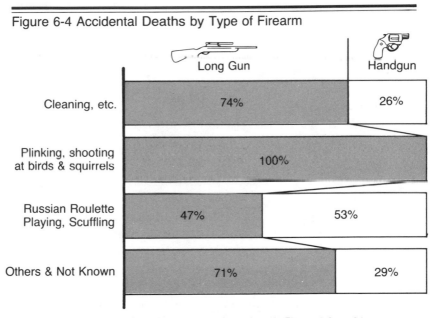

Figure 6-4 Accidental Deaths by Type of Firearm

	Long Gun	Handgun
Cleaning, etc.	74%	26%
Plinking, shooting at birds & squirrels	100%	
Russian Roulette Playing, Scuffling	47%	53%
Others & Not Known	71%	29%

Source: Firearms and Violence in American Life (1969), Figure 5-9, p. 31.

of handguns. But in general, the long-term trend in firearms-related accidental death is downward. This is partly due to the decline in hunting accidents and partly due to increasing urbanization of America. From 1969 to 1978, there was a decrease from 1,100 to 700 in recreation-related deaths involving firearms in hunting accidents. Deaths in which firearms were accidentally used in the home rose from 1,200 in 1960 to 1,400 in 1970 but had fallen to 900 in 1978.

One of the most significant aspects of firearms accidents is the extent of the paradoxical costs involved. As we pointed out in Chapter 4, these paradoxical costs alone present a much greater risk to the household than any harm likely to be inflicted by invading strangers.

It should be added that firearms accidents also inflict non-fatal injuries. A survey of all U.S. adults in 1978, conducted by Cambridge Reports, Inc., found that 4 percent of the respondents had been involved in a handgun accident, half of them resulting in personal injury. Ten percent reported that a family member had been involved in such an accident, and 15 percent reported a similar experience for a close personal friend. In 1968 it was estimated, on the basis of National Health Survey data, that over 100,000 injuries were sustained annually from firearms. Wright, Rossi, and Daly estimate that in 1975 there were approximately 183,000 firearms-related injuries.

Firearms and Suicide

In 1969 the National Commission on the Causes and Prevention of Violence Task Force on Firearms reported that over 20,000 Americans committed suicide every year and that 47 percent of those suicides were committed with firearms. Wright, Rossi, and Daly give the estimated number of suicidal deaths from 1960 to 1977 and note that "the number of suicides has increased from about 20,000 to 30,000 over the two decades." They also note that "an important trend over time has been the increase in suicides with the use of a firearm: from about 47% of all suicides in 1960 to 56% in 1977"; and that "the trend among women is toward increased use of firearms for suicide from 25% in 1964 to 36% in 1977." But, curiously, about these extraordinary developments they make no comment at all. This is curious because, unlike accidental deaths, in the case of suicide with the use of firearms it is not hundreds but thousands of lives that are involved.

Little research has been done on the relationship between firearms and suicide, although the question whether or to what extent firearms contribute to the number of suicides deserves high research priority. It should be of concern that over the two decades from 1960 to 1980 it is evident that both women and the young have increasingly used firearms to kill themselves.

In the case of women the figures for the years 1960 and 1980 respectively are shown in Table 6-1; and the figures for those aged between five and nineteen years are shown in Table 6-2.

There has also been over the same period an increased use of guns for suicide by nonwhites, as shown in Table 6-3.

There is no doubt that for persons who seek to end their lives, firearms are a speedy and effective method of doing so.

Table 6-1
FEMALE SUICIDES
(UNITED STATES, 1960 AND 1980)

	1960	1980	PERCENTAGE INCREASE
By firearms and explosives	1,138	2,459	116
By all other means	3,361	3,905	16
Total	4,499	6,364	

Source: *Vital Statistics of the United States* (1960 and 1980).

Table 6-2
YOUTH SUICIDES (AGE 5–19)
(UNITED STATES, 1960 AND 1980)

	1960	1980	PERCENTAGE INCREASE
By firearms and explosives	304	1,214	299
By all other means	264	725	175
Total	568	1,939	

Source: *Vital Statistics of the United States* (1960 and 1980).

A study conducted in Los Angeles in 1957 found that as compared with other methods of attempting suicide, firearms produce the highest death rates. This raises a number of questions. Would those who seek to end their lives use other methods of suicide if all or some of them did not have firearms? If persons who now use firearms were forced to resort to other, slower means of self-destruction when there is a higher chance of intervention and rescue, would this result in a significant reduction in suicides? Does the presence of a gun and the knowledge of having a quick and effective way of ending life in some instances precipitate impulsive suicide attempts?

To these and other relevant questions we do not have answers. The National Commission on the Causes and Prevention of Violence Task Force on Firearms concluded its

Table 6-3
NONWHITE SUICIDES
(UNITED STATES, 1960 AND 1980)

	1960	1980	PERCENTAGE INCREASE
By firearms and explosives	427	1,112	160
By all other means	493	928	88
Total	920	2,040	

Source: *Vital Statistics of the United States* (1960 and 1980).

chapter on "Firearms and Suicide" with the words, "A person who really wants to die will find a way of doing so." This assertion is irrefutable in that anyone who does not find a way of doing so can be dismissed as not *really* wanting to die; but it is also totally uninformative. The trends in gun suicide that have accompanied increased gun ownership since the mid-1960s make us more inclined to suspect gun availability as a substantial influence on suicide rates in the United States. Information is required if we are to attempt to answer the questions posed above more definitively. The relationship between firearms and suicide is an important story waiting to be told.

REFERENCES

Boyd, Jeffrey H. "The Increasing Rate of Suicide by Firearms," *The New England Journal of Medicine* 308(1983):872–874.

Cambridge Reports Inc. *An Analysis of Public Attitudes Towards Handgun Control.* Mimeographed. Cambridge, Mass.: Cambridge Reports, Inc., 1978.

Farberow, Norman L., and Edwin S. Schneidman. *The Cry for Help.* New York: McGraw-Hill, 1961.

Newton, George D., Jr., and Franklin E. Zimring. *Firearms and Violence in American Life: A Staff Report Submitted to the National Commission on the Causes and Prevention of Violence.* Washington, D.C.: National Commission on the Causes and Prevention of Violence, 1969.

Rushforth, Norman B., Charles S. Hirsch, and Amasa B. Ford, et al. "Accidental Firearm Fatalities in a Metropolitan County (1958 1973)," *American Journal of Epidemiology* 100(1974):499–505.

Vital Statistics of the United States, 1960 and 1980. Washington, D.C.: U.S. Government Printing Office.

Wright, James D., Peter H. Rossi, and Kathleen Daly. *Under the Gun: Weapons, Crime, and Violence in America.* New York: Aldine, 1983.

PART

2

Gun
Ownership
and Use

7

America as a Gun Culture

Some years ago Richard Hofstadter, one of our most eminent historians, in a well-known article whose title we have borrowed for this chapter, wrote:

> The United States is the only modern industrial urban nation that persists in maintaining a gun culture. It is the only industrial nation in which the possession of rifles, shotguns, and handguns is lawfully prevalent among large numbers of its population. It is the only such nation that has been

impelled in recent years to agonize at length about its own disposition toward violence and to set up a commission to examine it, the only nation so attached to the supposed "right" to bear arms that its laws abet assassins, professional criminals, berserk murderers, and political terrorists at the expense of the orderly population—and yet it remains, and is apparently determined to remain, the most passive of all the major countries in the matter of gun control.

More recently, Wright, Rossi, and Daly have also noted "the unique role of the gun in American culture" and "the omnipresence of guns and gun imagery in our popular culture and myth." Remarking that it is possible to quarrel with some of the details of Hofstadter's depiction of America as a gun culture, they register agreement with "its general thrust." "The Gun," they say, "may not constitute the very heart of American culture and civilization, but it is assuredly an important component."

Hofstadter's observations on "the persistence of the American gun culture" are of interest here because of their policy implications. In his view, America's "inability to arrive at satisfactory controls for guns" was directly related to "the tenacity of our gun culture." Although he favored strict gun controls, he was deeply pessimistic about the likelihood of their being achieved.

His pessimism was reinforced by the fact that although in 1968, after the assassinations of Robert F. Kennedy and Martin Luther King, Jr., "there was an almost touching national revulsion against our own gun culture . . . [a] moment of acute concern," the moment passed without any serious gun control measure being introduced. "A nation that could not devise a system of gun control after its experiences of the 1960's, and at a moment of profound popular revulsion against guns," he said," is not likely to get such a system in the calculable future."

It would be idle to deny that firearms ownership in the

United States has been a feature of the American tradition. The Report of the National Commission on the Causes and Prevention of Violence Task Force on Firearms and Violence opens with the words:

> Firearms have long been an important part of American life. For many years the armed citizen-soldier was the country's first line of defense; the "Kentucky" long rifle opened the frontier; the Winchester repeater "won the West"; and the Colt revolver "made men equal."
> Firearms no longer play a significant role in keeping food on American tables, yet Americans own and use firearms to a degree that puzzles many observers. If our frontier has disappeared, our frontier tradition remains.

Here we consider briefly three questions. First, with the demands and necessities of frontier life long gone even from our rural areas, what role does the "frontier tradition" play in gun ownership and use in contemporary American life? Second, to what extent is it true that America is a gun culture? Third, what are the political implications of the answers to those questions?

The Frontier

To the first of these questions, Hofstadter himself gave the beginning of an answer. "It is very easy in interpreting American history," he wrote, "to give the credit and the blame for almost everything to the frontier, and certainly this temptation is particularly strong where guns are concerned." But America in 1970, he pointed out, had

> a culture in which only about 4% of the country's workers now make their living from farming, a culture that for the last century and a half has had only a tiny fragment of its population actually in contact with a frontier, that, in fact, has not known a true frontier for three generations.

He concluded that "when the frontier and its ramifications are given their due, they fall far short of explaining the persistence of the American gun culture."

It seems likely that the truth regarding the so-called frontier tradition is that nostalgic reference back to a less complex, more picturesque, agricultural or rural state of development is common to all modern, urban, industrial nations. And if that past featured a frontier, as it did in Canada and Australia as well as in America, that pioneering experience is inevitably incorporated in the popular stereotype of "the good old days." Similarly, all mass cultures have popular quasi-mythical folk heroes from the past (in Australia, such figures as Ned Kelly and Captain Starlight are the counterparts of America's Jesse James and the Dalton brothers) who were usually criminal and invariably violent.

It is sometimes suggested that Westerns and crime movies, which commonly portray the swift solution of all conflicts as being achieved with guns, provide some kind of index to American culture and exemplify "America's romance with the gun." This is about as plausible as suggesting that Ian Fleming's James Bond, with his 007 license to kill, and the movies featuring him typify English culture. Western movies are universally popular and provide vicarious pleasure, both in undeveloped and in developed, technologically advanced societies throughout the world. Some of the most popular were, in fact, made by an Italian director, Sergio Leone, in Italy: the so-called spaghetti westerns.

Those who remember Rap Brown's dictum (according to Hofstadter, "one of the memorable utterances of our time") that "violence is necessary and it's as American as cherry pie" perhaps forget that cherry pie did not originate in, nor has its popularity ever been confined to, America. Possibly they also forget that it was not an American but a European regime that, earlier in this century, celebrated the necessity for violence in a fashion and on a scale unprecedented in the history of mankind.

"The Gun"

Wright, Rossi, and Daly, as we have noted, approve the "general thrust" of Richard Hofstadter's depiction of American culture as one "where The Gun plays a central symbolic role, and quite possibly, the only such culture on the planet today." But when they come to review the available evidence on the characteristics of the people and households that possess weaponry, it becomes apparent that Hofstadter's holistic view of American culture overlooks some important distinctions.

The most critical distinction concerns the reasons that a weapon is owned: whether for sport and recreation or for protection and self-defense. The available research, they discover, "strongly suggests that the characteristics of people who own weapons for sport and recreational purposes differ sharply from the characteristics of people who own protective or defensive weaponry." Indeed, the "data strongly suggest that there are two distinct gun cultures—the first and substantially the larger being a culture of sport and recreation, and the second being a 'culture' of defense."

In fact, the authors of the studies from which these conclusions are drawn find "only partial evidence of a subculture of protective gun ownership." But what the data do most strongly suggest is that to talk of "the centrality of 'The Gun' " in American culture is grossly misleading. In the first place, the weapons possessed for sport and recreation purposes are predominantly shoulder weapons and long guns, whereas those possessed for purposes of protection or self-defense are predominantly handguns. And there is no "unique role . . . in American culture" that is shared by both types of weapons. In this regard, it is important to note that handgun ownership in urban areas, the key element of defensive gun culture, is a relatively recent phenomenon. How something that increased dramatically in cities in the 1960s can be blamed on nineteenth-century rural traditions has not yet been explained to our satisfaction.

In the second place, the fact that large numbers of Americans own a variety of weapons for a variety of reasons, including illicit criminal purposes (which might presumably be seen as yet another subcultural category), does not constitute evidence that the United States is a gun culture. It might more plausibly be suggested that because Americans own, per capita, more automobiles than the citizens of any other country in the world, America should be regarded as an automobile culture, whatever that might mean. Cars are far more pervasive than guns in the United States.

The notion that "The Gun" plays a central symbolic role and is omnipresent in all the ideas, customs, skills, and arts that comprise American culture is in fact nonsense. But the fact that it is seen as playing such a role both by those most firmly in favor of, and those most strongly opposed to, stricter control on the ownership and use of firearms does tell us something about the distortions of vision and judgment produced by partisanship.

Conclusion

What are the political implications of this analysis? It certainly provides little support for Hofstadter's conclusion that, because of the "gun culture," America is unlikely to achieve an effective system of gun control in the calculable future. Unquestionably, myths of various kinds exert powerful influences in political life irrespective of their truth value. But in the case of the gun culture myth, which not only excites enthusiasm but also engenders revulsion, it is impossible to determine what the nature or extent of that influence might be.

However, the question remains: If it is not "the tenacity of our gun culture" that has prevented America from devising satisfactory controls for guns, why is it that this country remains "the most passive of all the major countries in the matter of gun control"? Interestingly, in the final paragraph of his article Hofstadter offers another explanation, but it is one that appears to contradict his original hypothesis. He suggests:

> But perhaps more than anything else, the state of American gun control is evidence of one of the failures of federalism: the purchase and possession of guns in the United States is controlled by a chaotic jumble of 20,000 state and local laws that collectively are wholly inadequate to the protection of the people and that operate in such a way that areas with poor controls undermine those with better ones.

It is difficult to reconcile this explanation with the conception of America as a gun culture. We shall examine the chaotic jumble of state and local laws in a later chapter. For the moment it is sufficient to pose the question: How is it that a "nation so attached to a supposed 'right' to bear arms" should be afflicted with 20,000 laws—more than any other nation—many of these designed to restrict that right?

REFERENCES

Hofstadter, Richard. "America as a Gun Culture," *American Heritage* 21 (1970):4–7, 26–34.

Lizotte, Alan J., and David J. Bordua. "Firearms Ownership for Sport and Protection: Two Divergent Models," *American Sociological Review* 45(1980):229–244.

Lizotte, Alan J., David J. Bordua, and Carolyn S. White. "Firearms Ownership for Sport and Protection: Two Not So Divergent Models," *American Sociological Review* 46(1981):499–503

Newton, George D., Jr., and Franklin E. Zimring. *Firearms and Violence in American Life: A Staff Report Submitted to the National Commission on the Causes and Prevention of Violence.* Washington, D.C.: National Commission on the Causes and Prevention of Violence, 1969.

Wright, James D., Peter H. Rossi, and Kathleen Daly. *Under the Gun: Weapons, Crime, and Violence in America.* New York: Aldine, 1983.

8

Patterns of Gun Ownership and Use

In the annals of the gun control debate the American gun owner appears to be a Jekyll-and-Hyde figure, a personage subject to transformation from a benign, upstanding citizen into a vicious, brutal creature prone to irrational outbursts of violence. The typical gun owner is seen both as a patriotic American embracing traditional masculine values and as virtual psychopath, unstable, psychologically insecure, and dangerous.

On the one hand, there are those like the National Rifle Association spokesperson Harold Glassen who see gun owners as, for the most part, paragons of virtue.

> Americans are known as a hardy and an active race. Interest in hunting, shooting, and similar outdoor activities has been a part of the national fabric since the inception of our country . . . the vast majority of firearms owners typify the American tradition to the fullest. They are law-abiding, patriotic, and concerned citizens.

On the other hand, they are depicted, as Wright, Rossi, and Daly put it, as "irresponsible, nervous, potentially dangerous, prone to accidental or careless firearms handling, or as using their firearms to bolster sagging masculine self-images . . . a demented and bloodthirsty lot."

Neither of these images tells us anything about the American gun owner, who is in any case a mythical creature: the one kind of citizen in the United States who owns guns and owns them for only one reason, whether it be recreation or inflicting mayhem on others. They do, however, tell us something about the nature of the gun control debate, for the respective policy implications of these two images are as dramatically different as the images themselves.

To supporters of the sporting Dr. Jekyll, the demands of gun control advocates seem barely comprehensible. After all, the only people inconvenienced by firearms control legislation will be legitimate sportsmen. How is this irrational agitation to be explained? The best explanation Harold Glassen can suggest is that

> a significant segment of our population largely concentrated in urban areas has little or no interest in the outdoors, hunting, or the shooting sports and is easily manipulated into rash and ill-founded support for stringent and unreasonable controls on firearms without either an understanding of those who do have such an interest or of the true nature of the problem involved.

To those who see Mr. Hyde as the authentic representative of the gun owners, on the other hand, guns are simply lethal weapons, not merely capable of causing death but actually causing some 30,000 deaths, including 13,000 criminal homicides, every year. To them it seems perfectly clear that steps should be taken to eliminate or drastically reduce weapon availability to the general population. At the very least, there should be confiscation of the present handgun stock in civilian hands and, as in some European countries, the total prohibition of the private possession of handguns.

Of course, the fact that the majority of American gun owners are neither genial Jekylls nor hideous Hydes does not mean that it is a mistake to formulate gun control policy in the light of the available information about weapons owners. In fact, any balanced view of the potential of different gun control options must start from data on current ownership and use of guns. It is important therefore that we review the facts about the owners of the approximately 130 million guns (an increase of some 40 million over ten years) currently in the hands of civilians in America.

The myth of the single kind of gun owner may be the ultimate oversimplification in the great American gun debate. In fact, there is an enormous diversity among the tens of millions of households owning upward of 125 million guns. And sensible policies toward firearms ownership require recognizing the different kinds of guns and different motives for gun ownership in contemporary American life. Rational policy-making must take account of the diversity in patterns of ownership and use.

The best sources of information available about patterns of firearms ownership in the United States are public opinion polls, although they inevitably provide an incomplete picture because of reluctance to answer questions about gun ownership. In 1968 a Harris survey conducted for the National Commission on the Cause and Prevention of Violence provided data about patterns of ownership at that time. Table 8-1 shows

Table 8-1
NUMBER OF FIREARMS

FIREARMS OWNED	HOUSEHOLDS (MILLIONS)	PERCENT
None	30.8	51
1	12.1	20
2	7.9	13
3	3.6	6
4 or more	6.0	10
Total	60.4	100

Source: *Firearms and Violence in American Life* (1969), Table 2-1, p. 9.

the distribution of firearms among the 60 million households in the United States as revealed by the Harris poll data.

About one half of the approximately 60 million households in the United States reported having one or more firearms. The average number of firearms for each firearms-owning household was 2.24. Since 1968 the number of households has grown substantially as a result of population growth and an increase in the rate of household formation to about 75 million. Whether this has resulted in a change in rates of weapon ownership or in the average number of weapons owned is not known. But there is no evidence to suggest that it has, and there has been an increase in weapons supply in the intervening years substantially in excess of the number necessary to supply the new families.

Viewed in the aggregate, then, gun ownership in America is almost exactly a fifty–fifty proposition. About half of all households report ownership of some kind of firearm, and the other half report no guns. Lying below the fifty–fifty split are a great diversity of factors that determine propensities toward ownership, such as sex, social background, region of the country, and city size. For instance, households headed by males are substantially more likely to own firearms than female-headed households, and males are far more likely than females to have purchased the firearms present in a household in which both men and women reside.

In regard to regional differences, persons residing in the South and West were most likely to own guns and those residing in the Northeast least likely. The type of firearms owned also varied considerably by region. Rifle ownership was highest in the West (35 percent) and the South (35 percent); shotguns were most frequently owned in the South (42 percent)

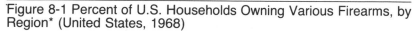

Figure 8-1 Percent of U.S. Households Owning Various Firearms, by Region* (United States, 1968)

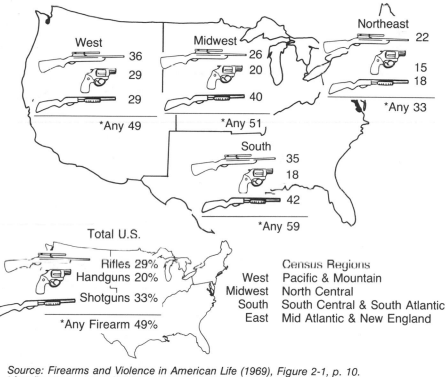

Source: Firearms and Violence in American Life (1969), Figure 2-1, p. 10.
*Any firearm = households having any firearm at all

and the Midwest (40 percent); and handgun ownership was highest in the West (29 percent) and lowest in the East (15 percent). The geographical distribution of firearms is shown in Figure 8-1.

Paralleling regional differences, the size of a community of residence predicts tendencies toward gun ownership. For all guns, ownership is greatest in rural areas and diminishes as place of residence progresses from towns to suburbs and the central cities of metropolitan areas. It was also found that shotgun ownership declines most rapidly as the population becomes denser—from 53 percent in rural areas to 18 percent in large cities. Rifle ownership declines less sharply—from 42 percent to 21 percent. Handgun ownership, on the other hand, is slightly higher in the large cities than in rural areas and suburbs. The nature of these variations is illustrated in Figure 8-2.

Figure 8-2 Percent of Households with Firearms, by City Size (United States, 1968)

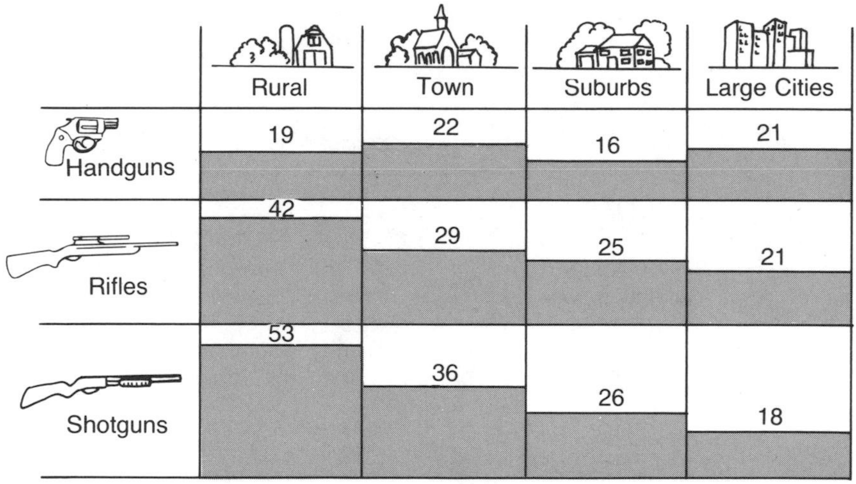

	Rural	Town	Suburbs	Large Cities
Handguns	19	22	16	21
Rifles	42	29	25	21
Shotguns	53	36	26	18

Source: Firearms and Violence in American Life (1969), Figure 2-2, p. 11.

The question of the ownership of guns for self-defense was addressed in Chapter 4, but we did not deal with the overall pattern of motivation for gun ownership there. Announced motives for gun ownership vary, with the most substantial reported reasons being sporting purposes and self-defense. Sporting purposes are the most frequently nominated single reason for gun ownership, but self-defense is listed as a partial motive for gun ownership by about two-thirds of gun-owning respondents.

Clearer patterns emerge when particular types of firearms are considered separately. The half of all American households that own guns again divides fifty–fifty with respect to handgun ownership. One in four American households, or half of those owning guns, report ownership of handguns. Although regional patterns of gun ownership are not profoundly affected by the type of weapon owned, handgun-owning households differ from long-gun-owning households not only in city size but also in motive. The mixture of sporting and self-defense purposes breaks down differently by weapon type. The overwhelming majority of long-gun owners list sporting purposes as the primary reason weapons are owned, while gun-owning families list self-defense or use in a trade or profession as the most important good reason for owning handguns far more frequently than sporting purposes.

As to the personal characteristics of the people and households that own guns, the most recent available evidence is ably reviewed in Wright, Rossi, and Daly's *Under the Gun* (1983). They note that although there is quite an extensive literature on the topic of the personality characteristics of private weapons owners, "virtually nothing of empirical substance is known."

As to how owners and nonowners differ in social background, economic status, locale, religious affiliation, and sex, it appears that relative to nonowners, gun owners are "disproportionately rural, Southern, male, Protestant, affluent, and middle class," but most of these relationships are fairly weak and there are "substantial numbers of weapons owners in all regions, all city sizes, and among all social, racial, and religious groups."

In short, there is no evidence to indicate that there are any such distinctive personality differences between gun owners and nonowners as the Jekyll and Hyde images suggest. And in view of the fact that about half of all households in America possess guns, this is hardly surprising.

REFERENCES

Glassen, Harold W. "Firearms Control: A Matter of Distinction." *Trial Magazine*, January/February (1972):52–54.

Newton, George D., Jr., and Franklin E. Zimring. *Firearms and Violence in American Life: A Staff Report Submitted to the National Commission on the Causes and Prevention of Violence*. Washington, D.C.: National Commission on the Causes and Prevention of Violence, 1969.

Wright, James D., Peter H. Rossi, and Kathleen Daly. *Under the Gun: Weapons, Crime, and Violence in America*. New York: Aldine, 1983.

A Domestic
Arms Race?
Gun Sales and
Use in the
1960s and 1970s

This chapter tells the story of an argument about the motives for acquiring handguns that is important in its own right and an example of rhetorical excess in the gun control debate. We begin with a review of the Violence Commission Task Force on Firearms findings on trends in gun ownership and then summarize a critique of these findings in later literature.

In 1968 the Task Force on Firearms estimated that the total number of firearms owned by civilians in the United States

Figure 9-1 Estimated Number of Firearms in Civilian Hands (United States, 1968)

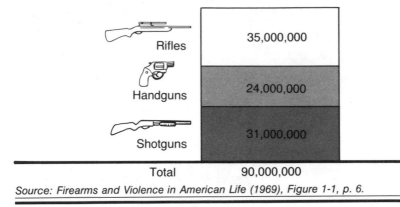

Rifles	35,000,000
Handguns	24,000,000
Shotguns	31,000,000
Total	90,000,000

Source: Firearms and Violence in American Life (1969), Figure 1-1, p. 6.

was in the region of 90 million. That estimate is divided in Figure 9-1 into the three main types of firearms.

The Task Force also examined the production and imports of civilian firearms over time and paid particular attention to what had occurred in the ten years between 1959 and 1968. It was found that between 1900 and 1948 an average of about 10 million firearms per decade were added to the domestic supply. In the next decade, 1949–1958, the figure roughly doubled to about 20 million, and in the decade 1959–1968 it increased by another 10 million to about 30 million. The number of handguns added to the domestic market showed the most substantial increase. The average introduction of 2.7 million per decade in the first fifty years rose to 4.2 million per decade in the 1950s and to 10.2 million, or a million each year, for the decade ending in 1968. Table 9-1 shows the long-range trends in domestic production and imports of firearms for the civilian market.

A major detailed examination of domestic production and imports for the decade 1959–1968 revealed that the greatest expansion of the firearms market had occurred during the

Table 9-1
FIREARMS INTRODUCED INTO THE U.S. CIVILIAN MARKET,
1899–1968
(IN MILLIONS FOR EVERY TEN-YEAR PERIOD)

PERIOD	TOTAL	RIFLES	SHOTGUNS	HANDGUNS
1899–1948 (average)	10.6	4.7	3.2	2.7
1949–58	20.0	6.4	9.4	4.2
1959–68	29.2	9.6	9.4	10.2
Accumulated total in 1968	102.3	39.5	34.9	27.9

Source: *Firearms and Violence in American Life* (1969), Table 4-1, p. 17.

previous five years. During the first half of the decade the figures remained stable. After 1964 they rose sharply to an all-time high in 1968, about two and a half times the earlier level as shown in Figure 9-2.

No less striking were market trends for each of the three

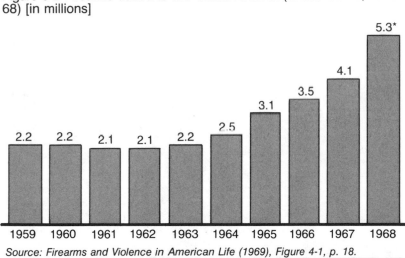

Figure 9-2 Firearms added to the Civilian Market (United States, 1959–68) [in millions]

1959	1960	1961	1962	1963	1964	1965	1966	1967	1968
2.2	2.2	2.1	2.1	2.2	2.5	3.1	3.5	4.1	5.3*

Source: *Firearms and Violence in American Life* (1969), Figure 4-1, p. 18.

major types of firearms over the previous seven years. Rifle sales doubled from 1962 to 1968, shotgun sales nearly doubled, and handgun sales in the same period quadrupled. The 1968 *annual* level was nearly equal to the average *decade* in the first half of the century. Figure 9-3 shows the market trends.

The Task Force Report states that to some extent the dramatic increases in gun sales reflected increased shooting sports activity. It notes, for instance, that between 1960 and 1966, the last year for which comparable data were available, expenditures for shooting arms and ammunition increased 72 percent—the same as the increase in expenditure for fishing equipment. But it says that although growing interests in shooting sports might explain much of the increase in long

Figure 9-3 Production and Imports of Major Types of Firearms (United States, 1962, 1967, 1968) [in millions]

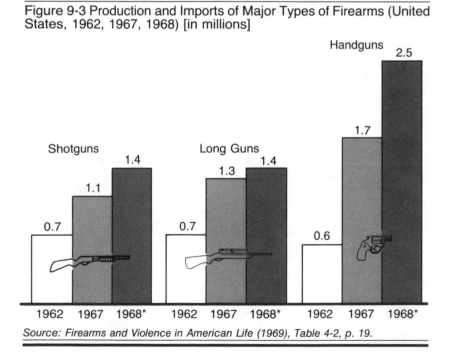

Source: Firearms and Violence in American Life (1969), Table 4-2, p. 19.

gun sales, it did not account for the dramatic increases in handgun sales involving 10 million handguns in the previous decade, more than one-third of all handguns produced or imported for the civilian market since the turn of the century. Fear of crime, violence, and civil disorder, and perhaps the anticipation of stricter firearms laws making guns harder to obtain in the future, are suggested as possible explanations for the dramatic increase in handgun sales.

Writing twelve years later, Wright, Rossi, and Daly note that production and import figures covering the ten years following the Task Force Report show an acceleration of the reported trends. They suggest that between 1969 and 1978 as many as 65 million new firearms may have been added to the domestic supply, roughly *twice* the number added during the previous decade. Furthermore, updated handgun production and import figures show roughly 2.4 million handguns available on the market *each year* (on average) since 1969, making a total increase of about 24 million handguns since the Task Force Report.

They are, however, extremely critical of the "anxious hand-wringing in pro-gun control circles" and the use of "typically alarmist" phrases such as "the flood of guns," "the domestic arms build-up," and "the domestic arms race." They refer derisively to the suggestion that the disproportionate increase in handgun ownership was due to rising fear and anxieties about crime violence and civil disorder as the "fear and loathing" hypothesis; and they refer to the Task Force Report as "by far the most widely cited source among authors arguing the fear and loathing theme." This hypothesis, they say, "depends on an extraordinarily uncharitable depiction of the motives and psychology of a very substantial fraction of the American population" and "suggests that tens of millions of Americans have, in the past ten years, gone out and purchased a firearm in the anticipation of possibly having to shoot somebody for some reason someday."

These remarks, however, compare curiously with what

they have to say elsewhere in their book about the ownership of weapons for protection and self-defense, for they acknowledge that " 'self-defense' is the most commonly cited for owning handguns." Moreover, they appear to suggest that the purchase of a weapon for self-defense is a perfectly reasonable thing to do. "[T]here is no doubt," they say, "that at least some crimes at some times and some places are deterred because the potential victim is armed." Indeed, this point is made at some length.

Thus, they argue that "it is plausible . . . that at least some potential robberies and burglaries never occur because the people who would otherwise commit them fear being shot by their intended victims." They also cite evidence "that the use of a weapon against a robber is an effective deterrent in some cases" and "that assaults are less likely to be completed if the victim uses a weapon than if no protective measures are taken." Why it should be regarded as "extraordinarily uncharitable" to suggest that such considerations as these have moved people to purchase guns for self-protection is not explained.

Their own explanation of what they would prefer not be described as the domestic arms buildup runs as follows:

> The gross addition to the weapons supply over the last decade apparently was within the range of 60–65 million weapons. Of these weapons some 20–25 million either were exported or functioned as replacements for weapons lost over the ten years; the initial net increase is thus on the order of 40 million guns. Of these 40 million excess weapons, about 20 million are accounted for simply by growth in the number of U.S. households. Of the 20 million that then remain, on the order of 15 million can apparently be accounted for by disproportionate increases in the popularity of hunting, collecting, and the other shooting sports. Corrections for these factors thus leave an excess of no more than about 5–8 million guns, of which perhaps one-half can be accounted for through enhanced arms demand

among the U.S. police. The number of excess weapons remaining to be explained by other factors is thus on the order of 5 million guns.

It has to be said that this explanation is so far beside the point, as a response to the Task Force Report's hypothesis, as to approach total irrelevance. In the first place, the decade referred to in that report was 1959–1968, whereas the decade referred to by Wright, Rossi, and Daly in the passage above is 1969–1978. Even if their analysis of the distribution of the 60–65 million new firearms manufactured domestically or imported into the United States between 1969 and 1978 were correct, to project that analysis backward in time to the previous decade assumes a replication so unique that even those most firmly wedded to the idea that history repeats itself would find it astounding.

In fact, there was no such replication. What the Task Force sought to explain was the dramatic increase in civilian weaponry in the decade 1959–1968, reflected in Table 9-1 and Figures 9-2 and 9-3. More particularly, it directed attention to the fact that from 1962 to 1968, whereas rifle and shotgun sales respectively doubled and nearly doubled, handgun sales *quadrupled*. And nothing like that occurred either in the following decade or at any time since then.

The second reason why the Wright, Rossi, and Daly explanation is irrelevant is that it ignores the point made by the Task Force in a passage with which they preface their chapter on "Fear and Loathing and the Mass Demand for Defensive Weapons." The passage runs: "Growing interest in shooting sports may explain much of the increase in long gun sales, but it does not account for the dramatic increases in handgun sales."

The Wright, Rossi, and Daly explanation relates not to handguns specifically but only to "the *gross* addition to the weapons supply." It is true that earlier they have suggested the "sporting and recreational uses would definitely account

for at least some share of the handgun trend" and they mention in this connection target shooting, gun collection, and
"use against the snakes that one sometimes encounters when
traipsing through the woods." The reference is, of course, to
"the handgun trend" in the decade 1969–1978. Even if it
were correct, it would do nothing to explain the unprecedented escalation of handgun sales in the mid-1960s. They
nowhere suggest that there was at that time a sudden upsurge
in target shooting, handgun collection, or snakes encountered
in the woods. Nor is there any reason to believe that there
was.

Conclusion

The arguments examined here are typical of the rhetorical in-
temperance and inconsequence encountered in the gun control
debate. The attribution of the derogatory "fear and loathing"
hypothesis to those who formulated a reasonable explanation
for the extraordinary expansion in handgun ownership in the
1960s is unfortunately characteristic. In fact, it is undeniable
that fear of crime and violence are an important part of the
explanation of the salience of the handgun in American urban
life. If that were not the case, the problem of appropriate gun
control would be much less intractable.

The striking contrast between the handgun and other
weapons that emerges in so many different topical investi-
gations is also dominant here. The handgun is useful for a
variety of purposes, but there is no doubt that it is most commonly thought of as a means of self-defense. It is utterly un-
surprising, therefore, that variations in the perceived need for
self-protection should play an important role in generating
fluctuations in handgun sales. What is remarkable is that this
should be the subject of controversy.

REFERENCES

Newton, George D., Jr., and Franklin E. Zimring. *Firearms and Violence in American Life: A Staff Report Submitted to the National Commission on the Causes and Prevention of Violence.* Washington, D.C.: National Commission on the Causes and Prevention of Violence, 1969.

Wright, James D., Peter H. Rossi, and Kathleen Daly. *Under the Gun: Weapons, Crime, and Violence in America.* New York: Aldine, 1983.

CHAPTER

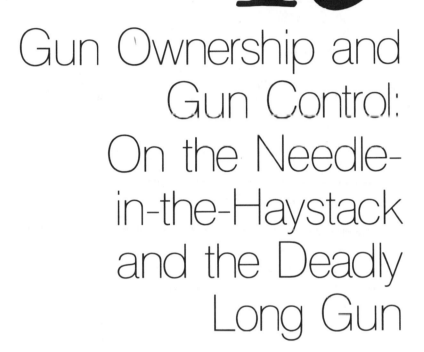

Gun Ownership and Gun Control: On the Needle-in-the-Haystack and the Deadly Long Gun

The needle-in-the-haystack argument is designed to minimize the potential of gun regulation to reduce firearm-related violence. It is argued that a general reduction in firearms availability would be unlikely to be accompanied by a reduction in the availability of firearms to criminals. This is because it is said that something in excess of 99 percent of all privately owned firearms are never involved in any sort of criminal act, and it is likely that the criminally abused 1 percent would be the last guns to be touched by any sort of restrictive weapons policy.

As Don B. Kates, Jr., has put it in *Firearms and Violence: Issues of Public Policy:*

> The conclusion that gun laws cannot dramatically reduce crime necessarily follows from the [finding] . . . that the vast majority of gun owners are responsible adults who neither misuse nor want to misuse their guns. . . . Even in a very violent society the number of potential misusers is so small that the number of firearms legally or illegally available to its members will always be ample for their needs regardless of how restrictive gun laws are or how strenuously they are enforced.

Currently there are well over 100 million guns in private hands and some 1 million gun incidents in any given year. Thus, the guns now owned exceed the annual incident count by a factor of over 100. The significance of these figures, according to Wright, Rossi, and Daly, is that the existing stock of guns now in private hands is "adequate to supply all conceivable criminal purposes for at least the entire next century, even if the worldwide manufacture of new guns were halted today and if each presently owned firearm were used criminally once and only once."

In these circumstances it is said that even if a national program of firearms confiscation were embarked on, it would involve confiscating at least 100 guns to get one that in any given year would otherwise have been involved in some sort of firearms incident, and several thousand to get one that in any given year would otherwise have been used to bring about someone's death. Moreover, these estimates are based on the totally unrealistic assumption that criminals would turn in their guns like law-abiding gun owners.

There is some dispute about the extent of the criminal misuse of handguns that is the crux of this argument. Wright, Rossi, and Daly say "it may be taken as *self-evident* that something in excess of 99% of all privately-owned firearms are never involved in any sort of criminal act," although they do not say why this assertion should be regarded as evident without need of proof or explanation.

Don B. Kates, Jr., makes this claim look like a gross underestimate. He claims that

> the ratio of handgun criminals to handguns is perhaps 1 to 600 (and of handgun murderers to handguns 1 to 5,400) . . . Thus making the over-optimistic assumption that a complete handgun ban would result in a 90% diminution through surrender and confiscation, there would still be 60 handguns left for every handgun criminal and 540 for every murderer.

On the basis of his figures, the existing stock of guns would be adequate for all criminal purposes not merely for a century but for something approaching a millennium.

In short, it is said that the number of firearms presently available in the United States is so great that the time to do anything about them has long since passed. Given the number of privately owned guns already present on the scene, even if some reduction in the general availability of firearms to the private market were achieved, it would have a minimal effect on the availability of firearms to persons wishing to arm themselves for criminal or illicit purposes.

Three points should be made about the statistics employed and the inferences that are drawn from them in the argument. First, the interpretations made are both inconsistent and wrong. For example, the estimates of the extent of criminal misuse of guns cited above are arrived at by dividing an estimate of the total handgun stock by an estimate of the number of criminal incidents occurring *in one year*. Thus, Don B. Kates, Jr., explains that his ratio of handgun murders to handguns "is obtained by dividing the estimated number of handguns (54 million) by 10,000 which, plus or minus, is the figure at which handgun homicide has stood *annually* over the past five years" *(emphasis added)*.

It is thus simply not true that 99 percent of all guns are never involved in crime. Instead, fewer than 1 percent of all guns are involved in criminal misuse *in any given year*, just as less that 1 percent of the American population dies of heart disease in a single year. But that does not make either heart disease or gun-related crimes a small problem cumulatively.

The *career* risk of guns being misused is very much greater. The available evidence suggests that probably more than 10 percent of all handguns are used in crime or serious violence, usually within a decade of first sale. This does not apply to long guns, a much smaller fraction of which are so used.

There is also ample evidence to indicate that the existing stock of civilian guns is nowhere near a century's supply for criminal users. Only by ignoring existing data on the firearms used in crime and also assuming that guns owned by anyone are freely available to all who would misuse them can the extravagant claims about "a century's supply" be given any semblance of a conceptual foundation.

Nevertheless, although the conclusions drawn from statistics on civilian ownership in this argument are fantastic, it is true that any balanced view of the potential of different gun control options must start with data on current ownership and use of guns and how these patterns might be affected by various policy options. Detailed knowledge of gun ownership, the determinants of availability to potential gun misusers, and the effect of controls on gun availability in the middle and long run are vital in assessing the prospects of different proposals for reducing gun violence.

The fallacy involved in the needle-in-the-haystack argument is the assumption that the available information on existing gun ownership and gun use in crime provides an adequate springboard for an inferential leap to a general conclusion. In fact, it can serve as no more than a starting point for analysis. The attempt to use that information as a basis for sweeping policy appraisals involves a substantial misapprehension of the nature of the problem of devising effective gun control mechanisms.

Another argument that is designed to minimize the potential of gun controls to reduce gun crimes relates to gun control proposals that are focused specifically on the handgun. It is acknowledged that currently the great majority of such crimes are committed with handguns. But it is suggested that a reduction in the availability of handguns could mean that in their absence much of the crime now committed with handguns would be committed with shoulder weapons, which are much more lethal.

Wright, Rossi, and Daly have this to say:

> We would do well to remember that there are already some three or four times more shoulder weapons than handguns in circulation in the United States, and that, on the average, they are much deadlier than handguns. If someone intends to open fire on the authors of this study, our *strong* preference is that they open fire with a handgun. . . . The possibility that even a fraction of the predators who now walk the streets armed with handguns would, in the face of a handgun ban, prowl with sawed-off shotguns instead, causes one to tremble. It can be taken as given that some people will continue shooting at one another as long as there are *any* guns around. This being the case, we have to muster the courage to ask whether we wouldn't be just as happy if they shot at one another with handguns [authors' emphasis].

Although there are other questions the authors might have mustered the courage to ask, or at least raise, they fail to do so. It is notable that they present no data on the death rate from various types of assault with shoulder weapons or sawed-off shotguns. Nor do they present any data on the degree to which rifles and shotguns would or do displace scarce handguns in the United States or any other nation.

Another critic of handgun controls who does not allow the absence of evidence to inhibit him unduly is Professor Gary Kleck, who argues in *Firearms and Violence: Issues of Public Policy* (1984) that if severe limits were imposed on the legal ownership of handguns, then the restricted availability of handguns could result in a higher death rate from attacks if more deadly weapons like rifles and shotguns were substituted.

On the question of displacement or substitution, he asserts that "long guns are eminently substitutable for handguns in virtually all felony killing situations." He treats *a guess* in the literature that the displacement to long guns *would be no more than* one-third as the equivalent of *a finding* that it *would be* a third. With regard to differential deadliness he says that "it would be pointless to compare actual observed assault fatality rates of handguns and long guns in order to determine relative deadliness, even if adequate data were available for such an effort, since the fatality rates are not just the result of the deadliness of the weapons themselves."

In place of deadliness he employs the concept of the relative "stopping power" of guns. Although this appears to represent an acknowledgment of instrumentality effects by one of their critics, the superiority of "stopping power" over the actual death rate is difficult to discern. Indeed, when it is applied to what is known about death rates it yields quite preposterous conclusions.

Thus, the use of this method results in estimates that some guns, such as the 12-gauge shotgun with double-ought cartridges, would produce fatalities in head and chest wounds about 18 times as often as .22-caliber rifles. But the death rate from .22-caliber, single wound attacks with a head or chest injury has been found to be 16 percent. Multiplying this death rate by 18 (the difference in relative "stopping power") produces an estimated death rate of 288 percent for single-wound attacks with 12-gauge shotguns that result in head or chest wounds, or approximately three deaths for every individual attacked! The death rate from multiple-wound .22-caliber attacks has been found to be 28 percent. Multiplying this estimate by 18 produces an estimated death rate for shotgun attacks of 504 percent, or five deaths for every individual attacked!

A critique that involves a comparison of the deadliness

of different guns but studiously neglects to consider the use of those guns in actual attacks, and entails death rate estimates of three per wounding, tells us nothing about the potential effectiveness of handgun controls. But its bizarre character demonstrates that in regard to this topic, even on the scholarly level, partisanship can engender strange aberrations. It must require a potent combination of wishful thinking, reciprocal noncriticism by peers, and absence of self-examination for this kind of catastrophic error to march into the public debate on guns and gun control.

REFERENCES

Cook, Phillip J. "Guns and Crime: The Peril of Long Division," *Journal of Policy Analysis and Management* 81(1981):120–125.

Kates, Don B., Jr., ed. *Firearms and Violence: Issues of Public Policy.* Cambridge, Mass.: Ballinger, 1984.

Wright, James, D., Peter H. Rossi, and Kathleen Daly. *Under the Gun: Weapons, Crime, and Violence in America.* New York: Aldine, 1983.

Zimring, Franklin E. "The Medium Is the Message: Firearms Caliber as a Determinant of Death from Assault," *Journal of Legal Studies* 1(1972):97–123.

11

Gun
Ownership
as
Victimless
Crime

An accusation frequently leveled at many liberals who favor gun control laws is that they are inconsistent, if not hypocritical, in that they both advocate the decriminalization of a range of behavior that they refer to as victimless crimes (for example, prostitution, gambling, and drug use) and at the same time recommend the criminalization through gun control laws of behavior such as possession of a handgun, which is no less victimless.

101

Whether or not any inconsistency or hypocrisy is involved, there can be no doubt that the pattern alleged is substantially correct. Thus Edwin M. Schur who, in *Crimes Without Victims* (1965), urged the withdrawal of the criminal sanction from such behaviors as abortion, homosexuality, and the use of certain drugs, has also, in *Our Criminal Society* (1969), argued that gun control could play a significant part in reducing violence and civil disorder. Similarly, Morris and Hawkins, in *The Honest Politician's Guide to Crime Control* (1970), both criticized the "overreach" of the criminal law and proposed an extensive program of decriminalization, and in the same book advocated the introduction of stringent controls on gun ownership.

An Intellectual Shell Game?

There can be no doubt that if victimless crime is defined, as for example Morris and Hawkins defined it, as "crimes (which) lack victims, in the sense of complainants asking for the protection of the criminal laws," gun ownership is a victimless crime. The mere illegal possession of guns produces no complaining victim. Yet, those who do not register their guns when registration is required or do not surrender their handguns when handgun possession is prohibited, will be classified as criminal although they have not misused their firearms or caused any harm whatever.

Furthermore, what are called the criminogenic consequences, which are said to result from the criminalization of certain acts, would surely follow if gun ownership were criminalized. Those consequences have been defined as: (1) diminished respect for the law; (2) unenforceability, corruption, and discriminatory enforcement; (3) the adverse effects of the elevated price of illegal goods and services (the "crime" tariff); and (4) misallocation of law enforcement resources.

A substantial minority of law-abiding citizens are firmly

convinced of their right to buy and possess guns free of control, and their respect for the law would be likely to be diminished by legislation designed to deprive them of that right. The absence of complainants would lead to problems of unenforceability, police corruption, and discrimination against groups the police fear or dislike.

The more difficult it became to acquire firearms legally, the more expensive those available for legal sale would become. Finally, it can be argued that the deployment of scarce police resources in a futile attempt to enforce the unenforceable would deplete the time, energy, and manpower available for dealing with the types of behavior involving violence and stealing that should be the primary concern of the criminal justice system.

Thus, it is argued that those who urge decriminalization of such offenses as criminal abortion, drug offenses, gambling, prostitution, and other such activities on the grounds that they are "crimes without victims," "victimless crimes," or "complainantless crimes" cannot consistently demand the criminalization of gun ownership. The concept of victimless crime provides no general principle that would justify withdrawing the criminal sanction from the former and extending it to the latter.

Further, if the criminogenic consequences of criminalizing behavior are supposed to provide a criterion for determining the legitimacy of criminalization, it is one that offers no basis for distinguishing between the offenses nominated for repeal and gun ownership that is nominated for criminalization. In short, the distinction drawn by gun control advocates is quite arbitrary and unprincipled, and they are "playing an intellectual shell game."

This critique is not entirely novel in that the decriminalization argument has in the past been frequently criticized for failing to demonstrate a general principle in terms of which conduct should or should not be made criminal. Indeed, we ourselves have elsewhere noted both a reluctance to formulate

objective principles and a failure to recognize a distinction between issues relating to the *morality* and *expediency* of prohibiting particular types of behavior and issues relating to the
efficacy of such prohibitions.

We noted that there was

> a tendency for the views expressed to vary as the subject
> changes from alcohol to marijuana to firearms to racial dis-
> crimination, and to vary according to the speaker's view
> of the rightness or wrongness of prohibiting the particular
> behavior under discussion. Commonly, the conclusion to
> such discussions is the comforting one that the law can
> succeed in doing right but will inevitably fail when au-
> thorities attempt to prohibit what should not be prohibited.
> Unfortunately, since there is a wide variation in moral views
> . . . this general principle leads to contradictory conclusions
> about the efficacy of particular attempts to control behavior.

A Prudential Criterion

In response to this line of criticism, it has been said that the
characterization of certain crimes as "victimless" was not intended to imply that there were kinds of criminal behavior,
or for that matter kinds of human behavior, about which it
could be stated categorically that they could not conceivably
in any circumstances harm anyone other than the agent himself. The distinction was not absolute, and no doubt most
crimes could be theoretically ranged on a continuum, distinguished from one another only by imprecise and indefinite
variations in the degree of harm occasioned to others. But although there would inevitably be disagreement about the appropriate placement on that continuum of many offenses, there
would be little dispute about such polar extremes as violent
predatory crimes, on the one hand, and noncommercial sexual
conduct between consenting adults in private, on the other.

The distinction was, as Professor Packer put it in *The Limits
of the Criminal Sanction*, "a prudential criterion rather than a

hard and fast distinction of principle . . . which brings into play a host of secular inquiries about the effects of subjecting the conduct in question to the criminal sanction." That prudential criterion has been defined by Professor Kadish as "if something costs too much for what you get, you'd be foolish to buy it." But he points out that there is no general "principle for determining how much of which costs are too much for which benefits . . . The [decriminalization] argument asserts the conclusion that the specified costs are too much for the specified gains and invites agreement in the hope that presenting a bill of particulars of the nature and magnitude of the costs may help to achieve it."

The crucial question in this context is: What are the practical implications of employing this criterion in relation to gun control? There can be no doubt that the enforcement of gun control laws would involve some costs of the kind mentioned earlier. Moreover, those costs, or likely adverse consequences, of criminal enforcement would have to be taken into account in calculating the relative costs and benefits likely to be derived from using the criminal law to restrict civilian ownership of guns.

What has to weighed in the balance against those putative costs is, as Professor Kadish has put it, "the objective of gun control laws [the saving of human lives] and the chances that gun control laws would operate to achieve that goal." Thus, anyone who reaches the conclusion, in the light of these considerations, that in the case of gun control the benefits would outweigh the costs, can without any inconsistency or hypocrisy support the criminalization of gun ownership while at the same time advocating the repeal of criminal laws in relation to other victimless crimes.

Conclusion

The discussion of gun ownership as victimless crime is of value in two respects. First, it is an useful discipline for those who favor gun control in whatever form to be forced to view it through the lens of the victimless crime categorization. The function of the victimless crime designation in criminal justice analysis is to alert observers to the necessity of thinking in terms of a calculus of the relative costs and benefits derived from using the criminal law in a particular area. It is as useful in relation to gun ownership as it is in relation to all the other types of conduct thought to be victimless. One would thus be ill-advised to support any measure to firearms control without paying careful attention to the policy considerations that underlie the "victimless crime" concept.

Second, discussion of the application of the "victimless crime" label to gun ownership provides a valuable tutorial on the meaning and limits of the victimless crime category. Those who regard inclusion in that category as justifying conclusive rejection of criminal law enforcement in relation to any type of conduct so labeled are forced to consider the implications of that kind of facile legislation by labeling.

For the rest of us it provides a reminder that the formulation of criminal justice policy in relation to victimless behavior requires the same complex and laborious analysis, involving both the estimation of unknown quantities and the valuation of different harms, as it does in relation to all the other categories of behavior we might seek to regulate in our society.

REFERENCES

Junker, John M. "Criminalization and Criminogenesis." *UCLA Law Review* 19 (1972):697–714.

Kadish, Sanford H. "More on Overcriminalization: A Reply to Professor Junker." *UCLA Law Review* 19 (1972):719–722.

Kaplan, John. "Controlling Firearms." *Cleveland State Law Review* 28 (1979):1–28.

Morris, Norval, and Gordon Hawkins. *The Honest Politician's Guide to Crime Control.* Chicago: University of Chicago Press, 1970.

Packer, Herbert L. *The Limits of the Criminal Sanction.* Stanford, Calif.: Stanford University Press, 1968.

Schur, Edwin M. *Crimes without Victims: Deviant Behavior and Public Policy.* Englewood Cliffs, N.J.: Prentice-Hall, 1965.

————. *Our Criminal Society: The Social and Legal Sources of Crime in America.* Englewood Cliffs, N.J.: Prentice-Hall, 1968.

Zimring, Franklin E., and Richard S. Frase. *The Criminal Justice System.* Boston: Little, Brown, 1980.

Zimring, Franklin E., and Gordon Hawkins. "The Legal Threat as an Instrument of Social Change." 27 *Journal of Social Issues* 33–48 (1971).

3

Strategies
of Gun
Control

CHAPTER

Strategies of Firearms Control

Two Slogans

Any serious discussion of gun control strategies must face the challenges expressed in two slogans. The first of them runs: "When guns are criminal, only criminals will have guns," and the message is simple. The fallacy of all antigun laws, it is said, is that the law-abiding citizen will obey them, whereas the criminal will ignore such laws as he ignores other laws.

The laws will disarm everybody except the criminals. Any registration list on file will contain only the names of the law-abiding and will be of no value in deterring or preventing crime. Law-abiding citizens will be subject to bureaucratic red tape, harassment, confusion, and costs far in excess of any measurable practical benefit.

The second slogan runs: "Don't penalize the law-abiding, punish the criminal," and the message is a corollary of the first. Since there is no evidence that permit or license requirements or other restrictions foisted upon the law-abiding citizens have any appreciable effect on the ease of accessibility of firearms to criminals, legislation embodying such requirements and restrictions is both useless and unjustifiable. The kind of legislation that is justifiable and would be likely to diminish firearms misuse and gun killings are punitive laws increasing prison sentences and making them mandatory for persons who commit crimes with guns. These laws do not make it harder for potential criminals, or anyone else, to obtain guns, but the policy is intended to reduce gun crime by making it so much costlier than crime without a gun that potential criminals either will commit the crime without a gun or will not commit the crime at all.

Such slogans are useful if they do no more than provide a warning that reducing gun violence will be a difficult, complex, and expensive task. There are already more than 20,000 gun laws in the nation to match the thousands of gun killings. Why should gun laws decrease the rate of criminal killings when criminals, by definition, do not obey laws? Why should law-abiding citizens be punished because of what lawbreakers do? From the apparent failure of existing gun control laws, their opponents conclude that controls cannot work, while their supporters declare that existing laws must be better enforced or different kinds of controls tried. How are these various laws supposed to work, and is it likely that they do or ever will? In this chapter we review a number of different types of gun control strategies.

Place and Manner Restrictions

Most of the gun laws in the United States are place and manner restrictions. These laws attempt to separate illegitimate from legitimate gun use by regulating the place and manner in which firearms may be used. They prohibit high risk uses such as the carrying of firearms within city limits or in a motor vehicle, the carrying of concealed weapons on one's person, or the discharging of a firearm in populated areas. Such laws attempt to reduce firearm violence by police intervention before violence or crime actually takes place. Since there are obvious limits to the police ability to discover persons who violate place and manner laws and to prevent firearm violence in this way, these laws may deter only a limited amount of gun violence.

Stiffer Penalties for Firearm Violence

It is not true that the National Rifle Association opposes all laws intended to reduce firearm violence. In fact, the members of that organization have been among the most vocal supporters of laws that provide heavier penalties for people who commit crimes with guns. More than half of the states have laws providing for longer sentences for criminals who carry or use a gun while committing a felony.

In order to reduce the number of gun crimes, such laws would have to deter persons who would not be deterred by the already stiff penalties for gun crimes. Can the threat of additional punishment succeed? Despite the dearth of hard evidence there is no reason to believe that such marginal deterrence is impossible. Perhaps the robber could be deterred from using a gun if the punishment for gun robbery were several times greater than that of nongun robbery. However, the problem is a complex one.

First, is it wise to make the punishment for gun robbery so harsh that the additional punishment the robber risks if he injures or kills his victim seems relatively small? Second, it may be that the only way to make the distinction important is to reduce the punishment for nongun robbery. Third, punishment for robbery is already quite severe, at least as set forth in the statutes. How much more potential deterrence is left in the system?

The issue of additional deterrence is also complicated when the crime of gun assault, that is, an actual shooting, is discussed, because the person who attacks with a gun is already risking the maximum punishment of the law if the victim dies. How much additional deterrence can come from making lesser penalties for nonfatal attack mandatory? Proponents of this approach suggest that although the penalties for crime seem severe, in reality light punishments are often given. Granting the truth of this observation leads, however, to the further question whether the same pressures might not undermine mandatory penalties for gun crime.

There may indeed be some hope of reducing gun crime by increasing the gap between the penalty for that crime and the penalty for other crimes. At the same time, it is difficult to believe that such a program will have a major effect on the rate of gun killings.

Prohibiting High-Risk Groups from Owning Guns

Another approach endorsed by opponents of more comprehensive gun control is to forbid certain high-risk groups from owning firearms. The groups usually covered include those with serious criminal records, fugitives from justice, the very young, alcoholics, drug addicts, and mental patients. Nearly every state, as well as the federal government, prohibits some type of high-risk ownership. Many of these laws do not go so far as to make a person prove his eligibility to own a gun; the ownership ban is supposed to be effective because the ineligible person will be subject to criminal penalties if he is caught possessing a firearm.

That represents some improvement over simply passing stiffer penalties for gun crime, because the law attempts to separate the potential criminal from his gun before he commits a crime with it. If such laws could reduce the number of guns owned by people subject to the prohibition, they would indeed reduce gun violence. But trying to isolate a group of "bad guys" who cannot have guns from a larger group of "good guys" who will continue to own millions of them is neither easy nor very effective.

It is not easy since if the purchaser does not have to prove that he is not in the prohibited class, the law is still trying to use the threat of future punishment as a substitute for a system that would make it actually more difficult for high-risk groups to obtain guns. It is of limited effect because most homicides are committed by "good guys," that is, by persons who would qualify for ownership under any prohibition that operated on only a minority of the population.

PERMISSIVE LICENSING

Many states try to enforce the ban on gun ownership by high-risk groups by requiring that people qualify themselves before they can buy guns. This type of restriction takes one of two forms: a license to buy a gun, or an application to purchase coupled with a waiting period. Permissive licensing is thought to be better than a simple ban on ownership because it makes a person prove that he is eligible to own a gun before he can obtain a license. Such a system no longer depends solely on the honesty of the people barred from ownership precisely because they are not thought to be good risks.

However, such a system is also precisely where what has been called the "gun lobby" draws the line and begins opposing controls because licensing imposes costs on all gun owners. Would licensing work, assuming that the opponents could be outvoted? Like ownership prohibitions, it would not prevent the majority of gun killings, which are committed by persons who would qualify for ownership. But would it at least keep guns from high-risk groups?

The problem with permissive licensing is that it would leave, on a national basis, some thirty-five million handguns in circulation. Half of all the handguns in the United States are acquired secondhand, and most of these are purchased from private parties, who may not ask to see licenses. Moreover, there are 35 million handguns available to steal. In short, it is extraordinarily difficult to let the "good guys" have all the firearms they want and at the same time to keep the "bad guys" unarmed.

It does not appear that states with permissive licensing systems made much progress in reducing gun violence during all the years when the federal government failed to control interstate traffic in most firearms. With stronger federal aid, the potential of such laws is still limited, but it is not known to what extent.

REGISTRATION

Under this procedure, the fact that a particular gun is the property of a particular licensed owner is recorded. Several states and cities have such registration laws, often coupled with other types of gun controls. Gun registration usually requires that the owner provide information about the guns he owns, in addition to the information about himself that is required to obtain a license. An analogy to the registration system for automobiles is often drawn by supporters of such controls.

For reasons that are at least partly obscure, registration is one of the most feared of all types of gun control laws, and the one that the gun owners find hardest to understand. The fear is based in part on anxieties about "Big Brother" keeping information about details of personal life.

The best argument against registration is clearly its cost, but the debate centers on the purpose of registration. If criminals—who, it must be remembered, do not obey the law— fail to register their guns, how can registration possibly reduce gun crime? The answer usually offered is that registration is designed only as a support to any system that seeks to allow some people, but not others, to own guns.

If such a system is to prove workable, then some method must be found to keep guns where they are permitted by making each legitimate gun owner responsible for each gun he owns. After all, some of the "good guys" would otherwise pass on guns through the secondhand market to "bad guys" and thus frustrate permissive licensing systems. If registration helped to keep the "good guys" good, it could help prevent gun violence, even if not a single criminal were polite enough to register his gun.

There is also a theory that gun registration will deter the qualified owner from misusing his gun, since it can be traced to him, but this seems less likely. All in all, it is difficult to estimate how much additional prevention a licensing system obtains by requiring registration, but it seems perverse not to require registration of some kind in any system that seeks to prevent gun violence by barring certain groups from gun ownership.

CUTTING DOWN ON THE NUMBER OF HANDGUNS

The most extreme solution that has been proposed in the mainstream of the gun control debate is a substantial reduction of the number of handguns owned by civilians. This proposal reacts to the frustrations of distinguishing the "good guys" from the "bad guys" by suggesting that no one should be permitted to own a handgun unless he has a special need for it.

Two approaches have been enacted: restrictive licensing and handgun bans. Under a restrictive licensing system, a person who wants to own a gun must establish a need for it before receiving a license. Under a handgun ban, certain classes of persons (for example, police officers and members of gun clubs) are exempted from the operation of the law. Thus, a handgun ban is not necessarily a more restrictive control than restrictive licensing, depending on the classes allowed to possess guns. Moreover, handgun bans usually exert no direct control over the exempted classes, whereas a restrictive licensing system licenses those who would probably be exempted under a ban. A significant minority of American cities have experimented with either restrictive licensing or handgun bans.

Many gun owners doubt that such plans will work because "when guns are criminal, only criminals will have guns." Moreover, if handguns are illegal, criminals, it is said, will switch to other kinds of guns, a development that will not reduce gun crime but will spur efforts to confiscate all kinds of civilian firearms. Both of these arguments have some appeal, but both ignore important facts about the relationship between guns and violence in the United States.

First, guns are more lethal than other weapons. Thus, substantially reducing the number of handguns should reduce the number of homicides resulting from accidental weapon use and the use of a weapon to settle an argument, even though some criminals will undoubtedly continue to use handguns. Second, it appears to be harder than one might suspect for the handgun robber or attacker to switch to a long gun. For this reason, the average handgun is many times more likely to be used in crime than the average long gun. States that try to restrict handguns find that their major problem becomes not the long gun but the illegal handgun.

The real difficulty in restricting the handgun is whether any law can reduce the number of such guns in circulation enough to make headway against gun violence and, if so, how long this will take and what its cost will be. It is possible, by law, to put a stop to the manufacture of handguns at any time, but even if this were done, some of the 35 million handguns in the civilian inventory would still be killing people in the twenty-first century. Under the best conditions, collecting the vast arsenal of civilian handguns would be neither easy nor swift.

Americans do not live under the best of conditions—the very crime rate that makes many people want gun control also makes gun control extremely difficult to achieve. How many citizens would turn in their guns when the law took effect? How long would it take to remove the guns from the streets, where they do the most harm? Should urban households be left fearfully defenseless? Is it desirable to add yet another victimless and unenforceable crime—possession of a handgun—to the depressingly long list of such crimes that have already accumulated? These are not easy questions to answer.

From Strategies to Systems

A system of firearms control will involve a number of different laws, each with a separate purpose, that operate together. In the United States, different laws will involve different levels of government, with local law controlling the place and manner of gun use, most licensing schemes being operated eeither by states or by cities. The federal government is responsible for controlling interstate and foreign commerce in guns and setting national priorities. The task of coordinating strategies of firearms control, of course, is of central importance.

REFERENCES

Cook, Philip J. "The Saturday Night Special: An Assessment of Alternative Definitions from a Policy Perspective." Mimeographed.

Durham, N.C.: Duke University, Center for the Study of Policy Analysis, 1979.

Jones, Edward D., and Marla Wilson Ray. "Handgun Control: Strategies, Enforcement, and Effectiveness." Mimeographed. Washington, D.C.: U.S. Department of Justice, 1980.

Loftin, Colin, and David McDowall. " 'One with a Gun Gets You Two': Mandatory Sentencing and Firearms Violence in Detroit," *Annals of the American Academy of Political and Social Science* 455 (1981):150–167.

Newton, George D., Jr., and Franklin E. Zimring. *Firearms and Violence in American Life: A Staff Report Submitted to the National Commission on the Causes and Prevention of Violence.* Washington, D.C.: National Commission on the Causes and Prevention of Violence, 1969.

Wright, James D., Peter H. Rossi, and Kathleen Daly. *Under the Gun: Weapons, Crime, and Violence in America.* New York: Aldine, 1983.

Zimring, Franklin E., and James Lindgren. "Regulation of Guns," In *Encyclopedia of Crime and Justice,* Vol. 2, pp. 836–840. New York: Macmillan, 1983.

13

State and Local Gun Laws

Although foreign commentators often appear to be under the impression that in the United States government exercises virtually no control over the civilian ownership, possession, or use of firearms, the truth is that America has some 20,000 firearms laws—more than any other country in the world. This is largely due to the fact that gun control in this country has traditionally been a matter of state and local responsibility.

There are a great variety of state laws in the United States today. Indeed, the variation between the strictest and easiest state and local handgun policies in the United States is as great as the variation between the general pattern in the United States and other Western nations. A review of state and local law is thus an important part of the total legislative picture and shows why specific aspects of federal law are needed to support state and local efforts.

Varieties of Legislation

State and local gun legislation has a long history. It began even before the American Revolution, when the Colony of Massachusetts prohibited the carrying of defensive arms in public places. As early as 1813 the State of Kentucky passed a law forbidding the carrying of concealed weapons, with Indiana, Arkansas, and Georgia soon following suit. The State of New York's stringent Sullivan Law dates back to 1911.

An initial distinction must be made between laws that regulate only the use of guns—what we call place and manner laws—and those schemes that attempt to restrict the availability of guns or of some types of guns. Many states and most cities today have laws that try to regulate the "place and manner" in which firearms may be carried or used, but in the early days they were not always carefully drafted. These laws are the majority of the more than 20,000 laws of legend in the United States. At one extreme there is the Arkansas statute enacted in 1881, making it a crime to "wear or carry in any manner whatsoever as a weapon, any . . . pistol." Without bothering to explain what is meant by carrying a pistol "as a weapon," it goes on to provide: "Nothing . . . shall be so construed as to prohibit any person from carrying such pistols as are used in the army or navy . . . when carried uncovered in the hand." It would be interesting to learn what success, if any, Arkansas has had in interpreting, let alone enforcing, this ambiguity.

It is unlawful in Texas for anyone "to carry on or about his person, saddle, or in his saddle bags, or in his portfolio or purse any pistol . . ." This doesn't apply, however, to "travellers," and the Texas courts have had quite a time trying to determine just who is exempt as a "traveller." In light of this statute, Jack Ruby was probably not violating Texas law by routinely carrying in the trunk of his car the pistol used to kill Lee Harvey Oswald, as long as he was en route between his residence and place of business. Only when he deviated from this route, and took the pistol from the trunk of his car in order to carry it on his person, did Ruby probably violate Texas law.

Most often, state law prohibits the carrying of concealable firearms without a special permit and the discharge of guns within city limits, and may regulate the transportation of guns by motor vehicle. Forty-nine states now impose some sort of restriction on carrying a concealed gun, New Mexico being reported as an exception, and 21 states require a license for carrying a handgun in a car. The most extreme carrying law is to be found in Massachusetts, where carrying a handgun without a license, or a long gun without a special ID card, is punishable under the Bartley-Fox Amendment by a minimum prison sentence of one year without possibility of parole or suspension.

State-level attempts to regulate the commerce in guns were frustrated by the use of the U.S. mails to circumvent state regulations on handgun transactions prior to 1927, and to some extent prior to 1968. Not until 1927 was a ban finally placed on mail-order shipment of concealable weapons, and was extended to all interstate shipment to retail customers in 1968. In the half-century from 1930–1980, more and more states enacted legislation going beyond the federal government in regulating the transfer and possession of handguns. As the fifty states of the Union entered the 1980s, more than half of them could already be said to be regulating handgun traffic to a significant degree. By then handgun dealers in fourteen states had to be licensed by state or local authorities, and an additional eight states required such a license for all firearms dealers.

Besides laws relating to the "place and manner" in which firearms may be used, various states have laws that prohibit certain categories of individuals from possessing either all firearms or handguns. Those excluded under federal law include minors, felons, aliens, fugitives, persons of unsound mind, and narcotics violators; the most common prohibitions added by states are for violent misdemeanants and alcohol abusers.

Screening Handgun Buyers

More than 2 million new handguns are sold each year in the United States, but it is estimated that between 3 and 5 million handguns change hands. The perennial problem confronting state and local officials is how to prevent this arsenal from getting into the wrong hands.

A police check on handgun purchase is the legal norm in twenty-three states, comprising almost two-thirds of the U.S. population, and three of these states have a similar requirements for long guns. But state regulations governing handgun transfer differ in several important respects, as can be seen by analyzing the three basic systems involving policy in handgun transfers:

1. A permissive and open-ended licensing system such as that of Illinois, which requires a Firearms Owner Identification Card for the purchase of any firearm, whether dealer or nondealer. It is called "open-ended" because the ID card can be used to buy any number of guns over a period of five years. Illinois has a waiting period of three days for handguns, one day for long guns.

2. The "permit to purchase" system, adopted by eight states, requires the buyer to obtain a permit from local police before the actual transfer of the handgun takes place. Under this system, a new permit is necessary for each gun.
3. The "application to purchase" system, in effect in a dozen states, differs from the permit system primarily in that here police silence implies consent. That is, if the police do not intervene during the waiting period, the transfer becomes automatic. Waiting periods vary according to state, from fifteen days in California and Tennessee to such short intervals in some states that it is questionable whether the police actually have a chance to check most applications. The system is even more permissive in South Carolina and North Dakota, which require only that the police be notified *after* the handgun transfer—on the evident theory that if the buyer turns out to be ineligible, the police will still be able to confiscate the gun.

All but two of the state screening systems are considered "permissive" in that they exclude individuals from owning guns only if the authorities can give a reason why permission should be denied to a particular applicant. As a result, most of the residents of 48 states can own firearms without having to give a reason. Two exceptions at the state level are New York and Massachusetts. Both of these states authorize the police to issue a handgun permit only when the applicant can establish proof of good character and further proof of a good reason for having a handgun.

New York is also one of four states—Hawaii, Michigan, and Mississippi being the others—in which every handgun is required by law to be registered with the authorities by the owner. Under New York's Sullivan Law, a license must be issued to authorize possession of a handgun in the home; a different license must be issued to authorize possession in a place of business; still a different license is necessary before anyone can legally carry a handgun concealed on the person. Moreover, New York requires such an extensive investigation of the applicant that the waiting period sometimes extends for months.

Unlike federal law, which does not regulate sales by non-dealers except to proscribe them from knowingly selling to a nonresident, many states do not differentiate between dealers and nondealers in regulating transfers. Every "purchase permit" state requires a permit for purchase from a nondealer. Even states that do not require a police check on handgun transfer often forbid the knowing transfer of a handgun to a youth or certain other members of proscribed categories.

There are three main sources of guns for those who are intent on avoiding a police check: the black market, supplied by thefts; the secondhand market, supplied by nondealers; and under-the-counter sales by licensed dealers. Before Congress passed the Gun Control Act of 1968, it was also legal to sell or ship weapons from a state with little or no firearm control to a state with a stricter system. This possibility exists again for long guns after the Gun Control Act Amendment of 1986. State and local enforcement officials complain about weak federal regulation of licenses, incomplete state criminal history files, and the difficulty of regulating hand-to-hand transactions in used handguns.

The State and Local Gun Control Debate

In addition to the constitutional question regarding the implications of the Second Amendment, to be dealt with in Chapter 15, there are three other issues that have been the subject of dispute in relation to state and local weapons control legislation. The first relates to the state of public opinion regarding state and local legislation, the second to the effectiveness of these laws, and the third to the direction of current trends.

In the first debate, the argument is between those who claim that most American citizens believe that we do not need more laws governing the possession and use of firearms and those who claim that majority of the public favor either more laws or stricter enforcement of existing laws, rules, and regulations. Most often this debate is carried out at the state level or in city government. The public opinion issue is a complex one, but a review by Hazel Erskine of the poll data on the subject of gun control from 1938 through 1972 found that "the vast majority of Americans have favored some kind of action for the control of civilian firearms at least as long as modern polling has been in existence."

More recently, a detailed review by Wright, Rossi, and Daly of two large-scale national opinion polls conducted in 1978 found that "large majorities favor any measure involving the registration or licensing of handguns both for new purchase and for handguns presently owned." It is interesting to note also that while "large majorities believe that they have the right to own guns . . . most people also feel that a licensing requirement for handgun ownership would not violate that right . . . there is little popular support for the idea that gun controls are somehow violations of Americans' basic freedoms."

On the question of the effectiveness of the 20,000 firearms laws currently on the books, the opponents of such legislation claim that the great increase in criminal violence over the past two decades is sufficient evidence that gun laws do not work and can have no crime-reductive effects because they do not diminish the availability of firearms for criminal purposes. Those who favor gun laws point out that the increases in criminal violence cannot be taken simplistically as evidence that gun laws do not work. Rainfall is not determined by the number of umbrellas being carried, and the increase might well have been greater if no such laws had existed. Moreover, insofar as gun laws can be said to have failed, the obvious explanation for this is in terms of the inadequacy of those laws or of their enforcement, and the fact that they are not uniform across states.

In relation to the third question, opponents of gun control assert that the tide of state and local gun laws is beginning to ebb. Those who want to believe so point to the ordinance passed by San Francisco in July 1982 banning handgun possession by most of its 800,000 residents—only to be voided by the state courts within a matter of months. They point also to the action of California voters that same November in defeating Proposition 15, otherwise known as the Handgun Violence Prevention Act; and more recently the 1982 Kennesaw, Georgia, law that requires every able-bodied male to possess a firearm.

Those on the other side of the gun control debate dispute this. They point not only to the 1981 Morton Grove, Illinois, ordinance making it illegal to own or sell handguns within the village limits, which has survived five court tests, and the District of Columbia ordinance banning the sale and acquisition of handguns, which has been on the books since 1977, but also to the historical perspective outlined above. They point out that substantial changes in state and local regulation of handgun ownership have become the rule rather than the exception in those American jurisdictions that have reconsidered handgun regulation in the past quarter-century.

Currently, the proportion of the U.S. population affected by state and city firearms legislation is estimated at 60 percent by dealer licensing; 70 percent by acquisition or purchase requirements; and 66 percent by police check before or after purchasing a handgun. The historical trend is toward a continuation of the patchwork quilt of federal, state, and local regulation, with the states and municipalities assuming an increasingly important role.

In fact, the historical trend at the state and local level is pronouncedly toward further control, with special emphasis in the big cities on handgun controls. No state-level gun control system has been repealed or significantly weakened in the last twenty-five years. The defeats for gun control proposals are all radical proposals at the state level. At the city level, very tight handgun control measures have been enacted in the District of Columbia and in Chicago. Many other cities have tightened local controls somewhat. No city has repealed or significantly weakened a gun control scheme.

REFERENCES

Cook, Philip, J., and James Blose. "State Programs for Screening Handgun Buyers," *Annals of the American Academy of Political and Social Science* 455 (1981):80–91.

Erskine, Hazel. "The Polls: Gun Control," *Public Opinion Quarterly* 36 (1972):455–469.

Newton, George D., Jr., and Franklin E. Zimring. *Firearms and Violence in American Life: A Staff Report Submitted to the National Commission on the Causes and Prevention of Violence.* Washington, D.C.: National Commission on the Causes and Prevention of Violence, 1969.

Wright, James D., Peter H. Rossi, and Kathleen Daly. *Under the Gun: Weapons, Crime, and Violence in America.* New York: Aldine, 1983.

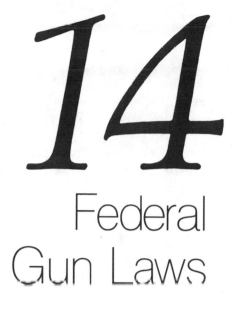

14

Federal Gun Laws

While firearms have always played an important part in American national life, gun control has never been an important federal legislative topic. State and local attempts to regulate the carrying of concealed weapons date from the early nineteenth century, with substantial legislative activity occurring during the period from 1880 through 1915. But there was no pressure generated to federalize the issue of firearms control until well into the twentieth century.

Urban crime and handgun use received an increasing amount of public attention during the post–World War I years, and this period produced a significant amount of state and local firearms legislation, as well as more debate about a federal role in gun regulation. By 1924, more than a dozen federal firearms control bills, most of them regulating interstate commerce in handguns, were before Congress. In 1927, Congress enacted a law prohibiting the mailing of concealable firearms to private individuals. This represented the first federal attack on "mail-order murder" but it had little impact because it was still legal to deliver firearms by private express companies after they had been ordered through the mail.

It is easy to overestimate the public importance of firearms regulation during this period. Although crime and criminals were major issues, there is no evidence to indicate that the "gun problem" and proposals to increase the federal role in firearms regulation were visible public issues. The first serious discussion of a more extensive federal role in firearms regulation came in the early years of the New Deal.

By 1932 federal solutions to many problems were being advocated with increasing frequency. Public concern with crime and criminals had shifted from worry about "highwaymen" or "thugs" to the machine-gun–toting interstate gangster personified by John Dillinger. The national fear of gangsters combined with the Roosevelt Administration's willingness to stretch the limits of federal jurisdiction to produce an unprecedented package of federal anticrime initiatives, resulting in a bumper 1934 crop of laws creating, among others, the federal crimes of robbing a federally insured bank, assault on a federal agent, and interstate flight to avoid prosecution for certain state felonies.

There were a number of reasons why a federal firearms control proposal could be expected as part of a larger crime control effort in the early Roosevelt years. The submachine gun, then of public importance, was a natural candidate for public fear and legislative wrath. It is also worth noting that

Franklin D. Roosevelt, as governor of New York, had defended that state's restrictive handgun licensing statute, had campaigned for a state ban on machine guns, and had publicly advocated federal regulation of interstate commerce in handguns.

The firearms control campaign of the 1930s resulted in two pieces of federal legislation: the National Firearms Act of 1934 and the Federal Firearms Act of 1938. The proposal that led to the National Firearms Act of 1934 had originally included handgun registration provisions that were deleted by Congress. In its final form it emerged as an attack on civilian ownership of machine guns, sawed-off shotguns, silencers, and other "gangster-type" weapons. It is often cited as an example of federal firearms controls succeeding. But although the use of these weapons probably diminished after it was passed, it is impossible to determine whether it had not reached an unnatural peak just before the advent of federal regulation so that the "Tommy-Gun Era" would have ended in any event.

The Federal Firearms Act of 1938 (FFA) was the most significant pre-1968 attempt to impose federal controls on the commerce and possession of a broad spectrum of firearms. It spread a thin coating of regulation over all firearms and many classes of ammunition suitable for handguns. The apparent aims of the 1938 legislation were to create an independent federal policy banning the receipt of firearms by what must have been thought of as the criminal class of society, and to aid state and local efforts at tighter control by prohibiting transactions that would violate local laws. As a strategy to accomplish these goals, however, the FFA was deficient in a number of respects, and was further crippled by a tradition of less-than-Draconian enforcement by the Internal Revenue Service.

The record seems to indicate that Congress got pretty much what it wanted in the FFA: a symbolic denunciation of firearms in the hands of criminals, coupled with an inexpensive and ineffective regulatory scheme that did not inconvenience the American firearms industry or its customers. Whatever

the faults of the FFA as a regulatory scheme, they went un-
noticed in a nation where violent crime rates had been de-
clining since the mid-1930s, and the larger issues of war and
economic recovery preoccupied public attention. Thus, the
period from 1939 (when the initial regulations under the FFA
were issued) through 1957 (when new regulations were proposed) was almost completely uneventful in relation to federal
firearms control. There was also very little legislative activity
on the state and local level.

It was not until 1968, after five years of debate and in the
aftermath of the Robert Kennedy and Martin Luther King, Jr.,
assassinations, that Congress passed the first comprehensive
piece of federal legislation specifically addressing firearms. The
Gun Control Act of 1968 was designed to "provide support
to federal, state, and local law enforcement officials in their
fight against crime and violence."

The primary role of federal law in the Gun Control Act
of 1968 was to help those states and localities that sought to
help themselves. There were five major features of federal gun
control under the 1968 law. It prohibited minors, felons, and
other designated high-risk groups from owning any firearms.
Bazookas, submachine guns, and other "destructive devices"
were forbidden subjects of private ownership. Importation of
what were called "Saturday night special" handguns was curtailed. The sale of firearms to persons who reside out of state
was prohibited to prevent states with loose firearms control
from frustrating the more restrictive policies of neighboring
states. And persons who sold more than a very few guns were
required to obtain licenses from the federal government as
dealers and subjected to controls and recordkeeping requirements.

The resources invested in enforcement of the federal law,
although modest, expanded greatly in the first years after the
1968 act. But the federal contribution to firearms control in the
United States made by this law was still not great. The 1968
act provided only modest tools to combat the frustration of

gun control efforts by the illegal movement of guns from loose control states to tight control states. No federal law prohibits the frustration of city gun control efforts by suburban and rural sales to city residents. (This is of particular importance because the most significant movement toward control since 1970 has been at the city level.) And the resources invested in controlling the flow of handguns by the federal government were not large throughout the history of the Federal Gun Control Act of 1968.

In 1986 a major new gun control law was enacted for the first time in 18 years, and only the second time since the late 1930s. Unlike the prewar and the 1968 gun control acts, the thrust of the new legislation is toward deregulation and this raises a number of pertinent questions: How important are the changes to gun control efforts by states and localities? And what does the passage of this legislation tell us about the prospects of gun control in the future?

As we have noted, many on both sides of the gun control debate see the issue in almost exclusively ideological terms. If one favors the principle of gun control, passing any pro-control legislation is considered a victory, and any step away from government regulation of guns is a setback. For anti-control forces, any cutback in regulation is a positive step toward that promised land where the ownership and use of guns by ordinary citizens is beyond the reach of government.

From this symbolic perspective, the gun lobby won a significant if qualified victory. In fact, the blunderbuss retreat from federal gun control passed in the Senate and proposed in the House ultimately was modified to preserve handgun regulation almost intact and to maintain significant regulatory power over firearms dealers. But if one's only criterion is whether the 1986 act was a step toward or away from control, that direction was clearly away.

But this is not the only way to view the matter. The legislation represented a great symbolic victory for the National Rifle Association and for gun owners opposed to both the principle and inconvenience of federal firearms legislation, but the practical impact of the changes is likely to be modest for three reasons. First, the gun owners by no means got everything they wanted. A vigorous if modestly financed counter-lobbying effort saved the 1968 law's ban on interstate sales of handguns, and moderated the cutbacks in dealer regulation that had been proposed in the House and passed in a Senate anti–gun control bill. The result was not a clarion call to de-regulation of the kind we have seen for railroads and airlines.

The 1986 act does not disturb the ban on ownership by high-risk groups, or federal prohibition of cheap handgun imports and the ownership of destructive devices. It does weaken the ban on interstate sales and soften dealer regulation. The prohibition on sales of rifles and shotguns to citizens of another state is lifted, but not the ban on interstate handgun sales. The recordkeeping requirements for licensed dealers are eased somewhat, but remain more extensive than before the 1968 law.

Every major regulatory strategy of the 1968 legislation remains in place for handguns, and the potential for regulating handgun dealers under the new act remains substantial at least for those persons still considered dealers under the law. If handgun control is the priority topic most gun control proponents insist it is, then the new law provides almost the same powers to support state and local handgun control efforts as its predecessor legislation. Further, the 1986 act, more than the 1968 act, makes a clear distinction between rifles and shotguns, the subject of the bill's most extensive deregulation, and the handgun, widely acknowledged to be Public Enemy Number One on city streets. Redirecting existing enforcement resources toward a handgun priority might simultaneously serve the interest of both rural hunters and big city police.

Second, the reduction in regulatory powers and record-keeping requirements need not be a disaster for regulatory enforcement. The circumstances surrounding enforcement of federal laws on gun dealership have been ludicrous for some

time. Under the 1968 law, substantial recordkeeping requirements existed as did extensive inspection powers, but the human resources invested in enforcing these provisions were
minuscule. Under the 1968 legislation, there was less than one
regulatory enforcement agent for every thousand federally licensed dealers, a ratio that guaranteed ineffectiveness. Reducing the number of dealers can increase the credibility of
dealer regulation.

In addition, the existing enforcement resources of the
Federal Bureau of Alcohol, Tobacco, and Firearms could in
future be concentrated strategically to help those states and
cities that are attempting to enforce strong handgun policies.
The number of foot soldiers assigned to the federal war against
interstate migration of handguns will not grow markedly in
an era of deficit reduction. In these circumstances, spreading
the criminal enforcement resources of the Bureau of Alcohol,
Tobacco, and Firearms evenly over fifty states is a prescription
for futility.

The final reason that moderate decontrol at the federal
level is not the death knell of gun control is that the crucial
arena for legal change on guns will probably continue to be
at the state and particularly at the city level. Municipal governments, particularly in the big cities, have been the most
active players in the firearms control game. This has been the
case for many years, and would have remained true if Ronald
Reagan had stayed west of the Mississippi. While interstate
and intercity leakage of handguns is a major frustration of state
and local control efforts, this problem is inherent in the Gun
Control Act of 1968 and not a special legacy of the 1986 act.

The testing ground in the 1990s for the costs and benefits
of restricting the availability of the handgun is the city street.
Major experiments are being carried out in places like the District of Columbia and Chicago. Limits on federal help to states
and localities have been a chronic condition of federal gun
control. The most recent legislative changes, unlike many that
have been proposed, will not make matters that much worse.

Some of the adjustments made in the 1986 act could help to rationalize federal gun control efforts in helping states and cities control the unlawful commerce in handguns. This would require close Congressional attention to the enforcement of federal gun laws, a strong commitment by the federal agency that administers the laws, and some shift in the polarized public opinions surrounding gun control.

In 1986 the gun lobby won a symbolic victory. Gunowners also obtained some relief from the burdens of federal regulation. Yet, it would be possible to accommodate these interests with a more positive federal role in handgun control.

REFERENCES

Newton, George D., Jr., and Franklin E. Zimring. *Firearms and Violence in American Life: A Staff Report Submitted to the National Commission on the Causes and Prevention of Violence.* Washington, D.C.: National Commission on the Causes and Prevention of Violence, 1969.

Wright, James D., Peter H. Rossi, and Kathleen Daly. *Under the Gun: Weapons, Crime, and Violence in America.* New York: Aldine, 1983.

Zimring, Franklin E. "Firearms and Federal Law: The Gun Control Act of 1968," *Journal of Legal Studies* 4 (1975):133–198.

15

The Second Amendment and the Right to Bear Arms

In October 1983 the Second Amendment to the Constitution of the United States once again made the nation's front pages. In its most recent gun control case, the U.S. Supreme Court, without comment, let stand a Federal Appeals Court decision upholding a 1981 ordinance passed by the Chicago suburb of Morton Grove, Illinois, announced as the first ban on handguns in the nation.

That ordinance forbids the sale and ownership of handguns within the confines of Morton Grove, population 25,000, and forbids handguns to be kept even within the home. It required residents to sell their handguns or keep them locked up at registered gun clubs, but exempted licensed gun collectors, as well as members of the armed forces, National Guard, and state and local police departments.

The Supreme Court order in the Morton Grove case was only one of about 800 handed down during the traditional opening of the new term, but it was the one that sent the press into action. During the days that followed, opponents and proponents of gun control were quoted at length as to the significance of the Supreme Court order. Indeed, the significance of the court's action was the only common ground shared by the pro- and anti-control commentaries. The irony is that they were wrong. The right to bear arms is of great symbolic importance to debates about gun control in the United States, but the legal issue of whether individual citizens have personal rights to firearms under the Second Amendment has been settled federal law for some time.

The Morton Grove ordinance had previously withstood four court tests: in the Cook County Circuit Court, which declared that it did not violate the guarantees of the Illinois constitution; in the State Appellate Court, which affirmed the Cook County Circuit Court; in the U.S. District Court, which ruled that it did not infringe upon provisions of the federal and Illinois constitutions; and in the U.S. 7th Circuit Court of Appeals in Chicago, which reaffirmed the U.S. District Court's ruling.

The plaintiffs in this case were seven residents of Morton Grove, with the backing of the National Rifle Association all of the way. Their argument was that the Second Amendment guarantee of the right to keep and bear arms is an individual right. The village responded with a "collective right" theory of the amendment: the Amendment guarantees the right of states to maintain militias. Obviously, differences of opinion about the right to keep and bear arms are an important part of contemporary debates about gun control.

The Second Amendment to the Constitution of the United States consists of only 27 words: "A well-regulated militia being necessary to the security of a free State, the right of the people to keep and bear arms shall not be infringed."

We will not here attempt any scholarship on the Second Amendment and the right to bear arms. We include a summary of the history and the case law to provide general background on this topic, and to show the relationship between these constitutional issues and the policy perspective discussed in the rest of the book.

The English Bill of Rights

The Second Amendment's guarantee of the right to bear arms predates the drafting of the Bill of Rights. Indeed, the origin of the provision may be traced back to early English traditions. The history is illuminating in that it reveals an interpretation of the right at odds with an "individual right" thesis.

Even before the Norman Conquest in 1066, English landowners were required to have arms and men constantly ready for defense of the king. These milities, or militia, remained the principal method of defense for the Crown until the restoration of the Stuart kings in 1660, when Charles II organized a large body of soldiers, paid out of the royal purse, as guardians of his court and person. He was prompted to do so by having observed, during exile in France, the power of a king possessing a standing army. The successor to Charles II, the Catholic James II, increased this nucleus into what Winston Churchill was to call "the largest concentration of trained full-time troops that England had ever seen." James II appointed fellow Catholics as officers, and deprived many of his Protestant subjects of militia status and the right to bear arms.

Incensed over these and other alleged indignities, a group of Tories and Whigs asked William of Orange for assistance in delivering the realm from James II. Four months later, William landed in England and marched unopposed to London.

The royal army collapsed, whereupon James fled to France, never to return. In the absence of a king, William set up a provisional government, and letters were dispatched to the boroughs and counties requesting them to send representatives to a convention.

This Convention Parliament, meeting for the first time on January 22, 1689, declared the English throne vacant. Three weeks later a Declaration of Rights, embodying Parliament's understanding of the proper roles of Crown, Parliament, and the people, was agreed upon and presented to William and Mary the very next day as a condition upon which the Crown would be offered. "We thankfully accept what you have offered us," William announced, and he and Mary were proclaimed King and Queen.

This Declaration of Rights subsequently became known as the Bill of Rights, a basic part of the law of England. It held, among other things: "That the raising or keeping of a standing army within the kingdom in time of peace unless it be with the consent of Parliament is against the law . . ." and, in the very next clause, ". . . that the subjects which are Protestants may have arms for their defense suitable to their condition and as allowed by law."

The latter provision is generally considered to be the progenitor of the Second Amendment to the United States Constitution. It is therefore important to note that the preamble to this act states the grievance to be the disarming of Protestants "at the same time when Papists were . . . armed." The rights granted by the English Bill of Rights was only such as "allowed by the law," and the law at that time already regulated firearms to some degree. The offense of "going about armed," for example, was founded in the common law. It was expressed in the Statute of Northampton of 1328 and in the following statute of Charles II: "No person who had no land of the yearly value of 100 pounds, other than the son and heir of an esquire or other persons of higher degree, should be allowed to even keep a gun."

Thus, to the extent that one looks to English or feudal history for the source of the American "right to bear arms," it must be recognized that a measure of government control over any such right has long been accepted. The first statutory expression of this right—in an age well acquainted with such limitations—was not to assert a right of individuals, but rather to assert the general right of the Protestant populace to remain armed in the face of religiously discriminatory impositions.

The American Revolution

Among the grievances listed by Jefferson in the Declaration of Independence, none had greater emotional appeal than those against the oppression of military rule: the peacetime quartering of troops in private homes, the superiority of military to civil power, the courtmartialing of civilians, and the seizure of militia arms.

Basic to all of these grievances, of course, was the existence of a standing army. Jefferson had already observed that the king had resorted to "large bodies of armed forces" to carry out his "arbitrary measure," and he continued this theme with his indictment of George III for keeping "among us in time of peace, standing armies without the consent of our legislatures." Rather than standing armies, the colonies preferred to look to their militias for defense, and any action by the king that tended to disarm the militia was viewed as an attempt to destroy the liberties of citizens. The British attempt to seize the militia weapons cached at Lexington and Concord led to the first important battle of the American Revolution.

No doubt, during this period there was also a considerable body of thought that individuals had an inherent right to have their own weapons, distinct from the rights of states to maintain independent militias. Many colonists were confronted by a wilderness of animals and Indians, and obtaining food often depended on sharpshooting hunters, but the disarming of individuals was apparently not one of the grievances leading to the American Revolution.

The American Constitution

With the British surrender at Yorktown, the victorious colonies bound themselves together with Articles of Confederation. These were weak laws, however, based on the absolute consent of all the colonies, and widespread disaffection led in 1787 to a Constitutional Convention, with the predominant mood favoring the creation of a more effective national government. During these constitutional debates, some delegates urged the adoption of a prefatory bill of rights.

Failing in this, they offered piecemeal amendments. Among these was George Mason's unsuccessful proposal that the grant to Congress of the power to "provide for organizing, arming, and disciplining the militia" be preceded by the clause: "That the liberties of the people may be better secured against the danger of regular troops or standing armies in time of peace."

When the Constitution was submitted to the states for ratification, the struggle between Federalists and Anti-Federalists reached bitter intensity. As a result, several of the states, although ratifying, criticized the absence of a bill of basic human rights. To remedy this, they proposed amendments to be dealt with by the first Congress. Massachusetts was the first to offer such amendments, but none concerned the right to bear arms.

At the Massachusetts convention, Samuel Adams proposed that the "Constitution never be construed to authorize Congress to prevent the people of the United States, who are peaceable citizens, from keeping their own arms," but even he ultimately voted against this. Among the amendments introduced by New Hampshire was the provision, "Twelfth: Congress shall never disarm any citizen unless such are or have been in actual rebellion." This was not adopted.

In the first session of Congress, Virginia's James Madison rose to champion a bill of rights, including this proposal: "The right of the people to keep and bear arms shall not be infringed, a well armed and well regulated militia being the best security of a free country; but no person religiously scrupulous of bearing arms shall be compelled to render military service in person."

This proposal by Madison was referred to a select committee, which reported it back in somewhat different form: "A well regulated militia composed of the body of the people, being the best security of a free states, the right of the people to keep and bear arms shall not be infringed; but no person religiously scrupulous shall be compelled to bear arms."

Though the House passed it in this form, the Senate changed the wording to what we know as the Second Amendment.

The Supreme Court Cases

Before the Morton Grove case, the Supreme Court had already had four occasions to construe the Second Amendment directly. Only one case, however, is a twentieth-century consideration of a modern gun control statute. Thus, *United States v. Miller* (1939) is the most important Supreme Court precedent. Here the Court upheld the National Firearms Act of 1934 in the face of the Second Amendment challenge. The lower court had dismissed an indictment charging interstate shipment of an unregistered shotgun having a barrel less than 18 inches in length, but the Supreme Court reversed, holding that the Second Amendment must be interpreted in light of its "obvious purpose" of ensuring the continued effectiveness of the militia.

The court said:

> In the absence of any evidence tending to show that possession or use of a "shotgun having a barrel of less than 18 inches in length" at this time has some reasonable re-

lationship to the preservation or efficiency of a well regulated militia, we cannot say that the Second Amendment
guarantees the right to keep and bear such an instrument.
Certainly it is not within judicial notice that this weapon
is any part of the ordinary equipment or that its use could
contribute to the common defense.

In more than four decades since the Miller case, a number
of lower federal courts have ruled against challenges to gun
control laws. One can argue that courts should regard the right
to bear arms as individual rather than collective, and that particular types of firearms should be the subject of individual
rights. But challenges to laws like that of Morton Grove can
succeed only if the courts change their minds. A ban on civilian
handgun ownership seems unconnected to the continued efficacy of a well-regulated militia. Even a general restriction on
civilian gun ownership might not contravene the terms of the
Second Amendment as it has been interpreted.

Whether judicial precedent on such matters is correct is
a matter we leave to others. But two less ultimate features of
the Second Amendment debate are worthy of special mention.
First, those calling for more expansive construction of the right
to bear arms are supporting a judicial activism many of them
oppose in other areas of constitutional decision making. Indeed, there is a neat role reversal in the mostly liberal advocates of gun control urging reliance on settled precedent while
many conservative anticontrol partisans plead for a radical judicial reinterpretation of this element of the Bill of Rights. It
is almost amusing to note the ease with which contesting parties can change philosophies of the judiciary when it suits their
other interests.

Less amusing is the tendency to translate automatically
questions of correct gun control policy into issues of constitutional principle. Opponents of gun control suppose that the
Second Amendment must involve a personal right because
they believe tight regulation of civilian gun ownership is
wrong. Many supporters of Morton Grove–style prohibitions

make a similar mistake. Decisions in such cases are not "victories" in the sense that courts have decided handgun laws are wise policy. That is precisely the question a limited system of constitutional review seeks to avoid. But the continuing acrimony over the Second Amendment shows every evidence of confusing arguments about specific legality with more basic questions of correct policy.

REFERENCES

Kates, Don B., Jr. "Handgun Prohibition and the Original Meaning of the Second Amendment," *Michigan Law Review* 82 (1983):204–273.

Newton, George D., Jr., and Franklin E. Zimring. *Firearms and Violence in American Life: A Staff Report Submitted to the National Commission on the Causes and Prevention of Violence.* Washington, D.C.: National Commission on the Causes and Prevention of Violence, 1969.

16

The Costs
of Gun
Control
Laws

In 1978 a private research and polling firm, Decision Making Information, Inc., of Santa Ana, California, which works primarily for conservative causes and candidates, was commissioned by the National Rifle Association to conduct a national survey regarding public opinion about various aspects of gun control. Question 25 in a 31-question sequence, administered to a nationally representative sample of registered voters, ran as follows:

As you know, about $20 billion is currently spent annually by federal, state, and local governments on crime control as for such things as police, courts, and prisons. It has been estimated that a national gun registration program would cost about $4 billion per year, or about 20% of all dollars now spent on crime control. Would you favor or oppose the federal government's spending $4 billion to enact a gun registration program?

The response to this question was as follows:

Favor	37%
Oppose	61
Do not know	2

Commenting on this result, Wright, Rossi, and Daly remark that although there is evidence that large majorities favor some sort of registration of *handguns*, this item "serves the useful purpose of convincing us that the public does not want a registration system *at any price*." It seems unlikely that many people would need to be convinced that the public would not favor a gun control system that involved the expenditure of astronomical amounts of taxpayers' money, but it may be that "us" is intended to refer only to the authors.

Would gun registration cost $4 billion a year in the United States? How do we know? Who might pay?

Although 37 percent of registered voters appear to have accepted the $4 billion estimate with equanimity and supported the program, the costs of gun registration have been estimated as much lower. A preliminary cost analysis of firearms control programs submitted to the National Commission on the Causes and Prevention of Violence Task Force on Firearms by Research Associates, Inc., in December 1968 estimated the annual cost of the record-keeping part of a national firearms registration system at $22.5 million (or 25 cents per firearm), which is roughly equivalent to $67 million in today's dollars; or $3,933 million less than the estimate given in the questionnaire. The high estimate is 600 times larger than the low estimate. How can such figures be so far apart? Isn't this evidence that all cost estimates are guesswork entitled to scant public confidence?

Nevertheless, the question of the costs of firearms control is obviously important. Any control system will necessarily involve monetary costs of administration and may involve such nonmonetary costs as inconvenience to gun owners and limitations on the use and ownership of firearms. That is why those who oppose gun control make an issue of both types of cost. And one important criterion for choosing between alternative gun control systems is relative cost. So making some sense of the cost factor in gun regulation is necessary.

Costs of Administration

In considering this question, it is necessary to distinguish between permissive and restrictive licensing systems. A permissive licensing system allows all but a few persons to have firearms and excludes only individuals belonging to designated high-risk groups, such as minors, felons, and drug users. Restrictive licensing assumes that relatively few individuals should be allowed to own the firearms covered by the system (usually handguns).

Both permissive and restrictive screening systems normally involve: (1) an application for permission to possess a firearm; (2) some investigation of the applicant; and (3) a decision whether the license should be issued. If the license is denied, this decision is normally subject to appeal. But restrictive licensing usually requires more detailed investigation of each applicant, including verification of the reasons given for wanting a firearm; and it may also cover the applicant's character and reputation.

Permissive licensing systems do not require exhaustive investigation of applicants. They need involve no more than a simple records check to determine whether the applicant is a member of a category of persons who are prohibited from having a firearm. The National Commission's Task Force on Firearms reported that "assuming renewals at 3- to 5-year intervals, a permissive licensing system can be operated for about $1 per gun owner per year, or a correspondingly smaller cost per citizen." In current dollars, this estimate might equal about $3.50 per licensed owner per year.

Restrictive licensing not only requires a more detailed, and therefore more costly, background investigation, but since it also requires the applicant to meet rigorous standards of need, persons denied a license may seek judicial review of the decision of administrative agencies more frequently than with a permissive system. However, the higher cost per application under restrictive licensing is usually offset by the smaller number of applications generated. After an initial flood of applications when a system is introduced, it is likely that the number of applicants would soon stabilize, as the standards for granting applications become generally known.

Despite the higher unit cost of processing, a restrictive system need not be excessively costly in the aggregate. New York City, as noted in Chapter 13, has had restrictive handgun licensing since 1911. A study of the New York City system found that the average cost per application of the approximately 20,000 original and renewal applications processed during 1968 was about $72. This was an unusually high unit cost, but it was calculated that it amounted then to only about 19 cents *per citizen* because the number of applications for the permit was so small.

Of course, the initial introduction of a restrictive licensing system would involve costs that are not involved in maintaining an existing system, and that is one reason Decision Making Information's estimate was 600 times as large as the Violence Commission's estimate. When a restrictive licensing system begins, many persons must give up previously lawful firearms. A schedule of compensation for firearms surrendered by owners who can no longer possess them lawfully would have to be established at the outset of restrictive licensing.

In 1968 the Task Force on Firearms estimated that if an average of $20 were paid for 22 million of the 24 million handguns in the United States, such payments throughout the nation would cost $440 million. If, allowing for inflation, in 1986 an average of $60 were paid for 33 million of the estimated 35 million handguns now in this country, cash payments would cost approximately $2 billion. But this expense would not recur, and in evaluating the costs of a restrictive system, it should be spread over a period of years.

Who Should Pay

Any consideration of the costs of gun control raises the question of who should pay for it. The unit cost of a permissive licensing system is so low that, even if all the costs were passed on to gun owners, the economic burden on applicants would be very small. With restrictive licensing, however, the high cost per application might involve economic discrimination or hardship if all of the costs were passed on to the relatively small number of applicants. This is because if the costs were too high, ability to pay rather than need for the firearm would become a criterion for determining firearms ownership.

The proportion of the costs of a firearms system that should be passed on to applicants in the form of fees and the proportion that should be paid from general funds is essentially a political question, but the answer to it could have a marked effect on the operation of the system.

In the case of a restrictive licensing system that is intended to benefit the community as a whole by reducing gun violence, it would seem only fair that people not owning guns should pay for a large part of the system, particularly when costs per application are high. A system with very high unit costs that imposed the entire burden of the cost of reducing the number of guns in civilian hands on gun owners would clearly be unfair and unacceptable.

Nonmonetary Costs

It is important to note that in addition to the funds needed to administer the system, there would be nonmonetary costs in the form of inconvenience to firearms owners and restrictions on opportunities for legitimate firearms use; and these costs would of course be borne by gun owners. In the case of permissive licensing the diminution in opportunities to own and use firearms would be minimal, but restrictive licensing could entail considerable disadvantages for those who now own guns.

In recent years, however, gun control proposals have tended to focus on the handgun, which has more limited sport or recreational applications, and if restrictive licensing were applied to handguns only, hunting and other shooting activities would not be significantly curtailed. Even so, handguns are used in a variety of legitimate sport and recreational ways, and existing legitimate hand guns owners would be adversely affected.

Thus, restrictive licensing for handguns would replace freedom of choice with a legal standard that would allow only a limited number of persons to have handguns. Target shooters might be permitted to store and use their handguns only at public or private arsenals or ranges; and collectors might be required to render their handguns incapable of firing. Most persons would not be issued licenses to keep handguns in their automobiles or homes, or on their persons. The removal of so many handguns from homes could properly be viewed as an added cost of a restrictive licensing system, for many handgun owners would consider it a great hardship to give up their guns.

Conclusion

Permissive licensing is an inexpensive system that promises limited benefits because of the high volume of firearms that continue to be available. Restrictive licensing, on the other hand, even if limited to handguns, would involve considerable costs, particularly at the outset. The monetary cost of an efficiently administered restrictive licensing system need not be excessive over the long run. Although basic information about the monetary cost of gun control is in no sense decisive in the choice between strategies, it can help to dispel a number of myths that have emerged about questions of cost.

REFERENCES

Decision Making Information, Inc. *Attitudes of the American Electorate Toward Gun Control*. Santa Ana, Calif., 1978.

Newton, George D., Jr., and Franklin E. Zimring. *Firearms and Violence in American Life: A Staff Report Submitted to the National Commission on the Causes and Prevention of Violence*. Washington, D.C.: National Commission on the Causes and Prevention of Violence, 1969.

Wright, James D., Peter H. Rossi, and Kathleen Daly. *Under the Gun: Weapons, Crime, and Violence in America*. New York: Aldine, 1983.

P A R T

4

Perspectives
on the
Future

17

Ideology, Crime Control, and Guns

A broad and distinct division of opinion exists in the United States on how to best address problems of crime, an ideological cleavage that transcends any particular issue. Whether the subject for discussion is police use of deadly force or mandatory prison sentences for serious offenders, youth crime policy or preventive detention, it appears that the same people are consistently at odds. Frequently, this division is characterized as a struggle between liberal and conservative ideol-

159

ogies. Generally speaking, those of the liberal persuasion are prone to condemn the system and condone the criminal. The conservatives, on the other hand, are apt to condone the system and condemn the criminal.

The striking contrast in crime control positions between former Attorney General Ramsey Clark, a liberal, and his immediate successor, John Mitchell, a conservative, provided a dramatic illustration of this ideological split at the political level. At a more sophisticated level, this division was reflected by the opposing viewpoints toward crime taken by President Johnson's Commission on Law Enforcement and Administration of Justice and the conservative attitudes of writers such as James Q. Wilson and Ernest van den Haag.

At the same time, however, there are anomalous features within both the liberal and conservative ideologies. Former President Richard M. Nixon, for example, while declaring that the only way to attack crime was to do so without pity, nonetheless expressed sympathy for the Watergate conspirators. Then-Governor Ronald Reagan said that the conspirators involved were foolish but not criminal. On the other hand, many whose attitude toward criminals is generally compassionate favored vigorous prosecution and punishment of those involved in Watergate. This paradoxical attitude of liberals and conservatives is also revealed in their respective positions on gun control.

Depicting the ideological polarity on the issue of crime control in the United States as a struggle between liberals and conservatives has some merit. Conservatives are more apt to desire the punishment of the convicted burglar or car thief. In contrast to this "hard-line" attitude, liberals are more likely to be concerned with the offenders' sensibilities. Moreover, it is often asserted that liberals favor the criminal, whereas their opponents are devoted to looking after the interests of the rest of society. And, while liberals strive to decentralize police power and expand and protect civil liberties, most of those labeled as crime control conservatives welcome policies that tend to center authority in the police, often at the expense of individual liberty.

Major difficulties are encountered, however, when one attempts to extend this hard-line/soft-line analysis to the relative enthusiasm of each group for the task of crime control. Liberals, for example, often seem willing to spend a great deal more money than their less-permissive brethren to achieve crime prevention. Moreover, on the issue of gun control, the liberal position seems wildly punitive to many conservatives, who, in defense of their position, invoke cherished individual liberties and the right of the law-abiding population to defend themselves.

The recognition of the apparent anomaly posed by the gun control issue is important, for any attempt to pinpoint and explain the ideological dispute on crime control in this country must take into account the fact that internal inconsistencies appear to exist within both the conservative and liberal ideologies. How can the lines of battle be so strangely drawn?

Sin or Social Disease?

A clue to the underlying nature of the differences in crime control ideology is found in the contrast between the way each party views the origins of criminal behavior. Liberals tend to view the origins with an institutional cast, noting elements that transcend the individual. They are apt to mention characteristics such as poverty, unemployment, lack of opportunity, racism, and peer group influence. Viewing the same situation, conservatives are likely to concentrate instead on the personal qualities of the criminal and speak in terms of selfishness, lack of discipline, lack of respect for and fear of the law, and occasionally in terms of the evil that lurks in the hearts of men.

Richard Nixon stated during his presidency that he totally

disagreed with the view that "the criminal was not responsible for his crimes against society, but that society was responsible." "Society is guilty," he maintained, "only when we fail to bring the criminal to justice." In a similar vein, Ernest van den Haag argues that those idealists and reformers who believe that "bad social institutions . . . corrupt naturally good men" ignore "the possibility that naturally bad men corrupt good institutions." James Q. Wilson says that "Wicked people exist. Nothing avails except to set them apart from innocent people. We have trifled with the wicked, [and] made sport of the innocent."

The personal/individual and the societal/institutional views of crime causation each have their implications for both the prevention of crime and the treatment of offenders. The proper method of treatment for an offender is closely related to and largely dependent upon which of these two views is adopted. Consider, for example, the long prison sentences that are recommended by "hard-line" advocates as a specific for criminal behavior. Frequently, severe punishment is justified on the ground that it is required to "teach the offender a lesson." The model is that of a pupil being submitted to an especially rigorous educational process. The lesson to be inculcated is usually described in such terms as discipline, self-control, respect for the law, or respect for authority. Because liberals, by contrast, explain criminal behavior as the product of social and institutional forces, harsh punishments appear to be totally irrelevant. How can one teach unemployment a lesson?

The Criminal Class

Another important dimension of this ideological antinomy is that hard-liners regard criminals as a class apart from the rest of society. As James Q. Wilson puts it, there are "the wicked" and "the innocent." "The true criminal," wrote J. Edgar Hoover, is "nearer to the beast than others of us." "The criminal brain," he said, works in a way "different from that of our own minds." On the one hand, there are the "vicious law-breakers" who are dangerous predators, and, on the other hand, the "honest citizens" who are their victims. Hard-liners are prone to attack as soft-headed judges and probation officers, who appear to be more concerned about convicted criminals than the innocent victims of crime.

Those who regard crime as the product of social conditions reject this division of society into two discrete groups—the lawless and the law-abiding. Criminals, they assert, cannot be clearly distinguished from the rest of the community. They point to studies of self-reported crime as evidence that participation in crime is widespread throughout society. As the Sutherland and Cressey criminology textbook puts it, "almost all persons have at some time deliberately committed crimes, often of a serious nature." The authors argue that it is a combination of adverse social conditions and the highly selective operations of our law enforcement agencies that creates the illusion that there is "a criminal class" preying upon the rest of us.

The personal–institutional disagreement over the origins of criminal behavior has, in addition to its differential approach to the treatment of the convicted criminal, spawned model crime prevention programs at total variance with one another. Viewing crime as a sin, the conservative speaks in terms of "fighting crime" and catching more criminals. The rhetoric frequently has a martial ring; politicians talk of "the war against crime." Society must be protected from the assaults of criminals by more effective law enforcement. The predominant emphasis is on the need for larger, better-trained, better-paid, "unhandcuffed" police forces.

Contrastingly, the liberals speak of a "cure for crime" rather than "a war on crime." They tend to regard the police ambivalently, as a necessary evil, and to view the prospect of more arms for the police with little enthusiasm. Basically, crime can be reduced only by fundamental social changes. Such things as the physical deterioration of our cities, economic dependency, broken families, discrimination against minority groups, poor educational facilities, and the like must be removed before crime will diminish.

The preceding analysis makes it possible to explain the apparently paradoxical attitudes of both sides on the gun control issue. Two things make gun control unattractive to traditional law-and-order advocates. First, the liberal demand for gun control is predicated on something other than the notion that evil intent is the principal cause of homicide. The conservative argues that few if any homicides due to shootings would be prevented if firearms were unavailable, since the criminal would merely select some other weapon to achieve this goal.

James Q. Wilson asserts, for example, that tougher penalties are likely to "contribute more to gun control than passing unenforceable laws calling for civilian disarmament." Ernest van den Haag argues that "outlawing handguns is not likely to be more effective than outlawing alcohol; zip guns are even easier to produce at home than bathtub gin." And, gun control is seen as something that imposes costs and controls on the honest citizen rather than on the criminal. This, from the conservative perspective, is not only pointless, for "crime is caused by criminals," but also unjust.

Two things make gun control attractive to the liberal. First, the characteristic emphasis on the number of guns available in the community is attractive because it suggests that homicide is a function of the availability of guns, which is a societal or an institutional matter, as opposed to individual wickedness. Second, the proposition that weapon dangerousness is the crucial factor in most cases of homicide, rather than any deliberate homicidal purpose, once again focuses attention on a circumstantial aspect rather than on an intentional or individual one.

A similar approach can be used to explain other apparent anomalies that exist within each ideology in areas other than gun control. White-collar crime provides another example. "Conservatives" raise the question, "Is 'white-collar' crime really crime?" The implication is that such "crime" is not criminal in nature. The white-collar criminal, it is argued, may be a violator of conduct norms, but his behavior is really no more than venial; as such, referring to him as criminal is mere name-calling, based on political prejudice.

The liberal also adopts an approach to white-collar crime at variance with his attitude to other types of offenses. Indeed, the phrase "white-collar crime" is denounced as "a revealing example of dual standard labeling by which actions are excused, mitigated, or trivialized by reference not to the nature of the conduct but to the status of the actor." The liberals say that large-scale thefts by deception or exploitation on the part of middle- and upper-class persons go unprosecuted. They emphasize that when they are prosecuted, generally more benign treatment is accorded white-collar offenders than traditional offenders.

Once again, this curious, apparent reversal of roles is explicable on an ideological basis, in terms of which neither party is really being inconsistent. For the conservative, crime is something that, almost by definition, cannot be committed by one's friends and associates, and, if it is, cannot be real crime. Viewed from this angle, the concept of white-collar crime represents an attempt to break down the "us" and "them" dichotomy. Nor is this merely a conceptual matter, because in practice some of "us" (law-abiding citizens) are, in fact, sometimes treated as though we were "them" (criminals).

The liberal, on the other hand, views the categorization of certain offenses as white-collar crime as a refusal to recognize that such offenses, and thus their perpetrators, are really criminal and that crime is a pervasive social phenomenon that is not a reflector of wealth, power, or class. It is argued therefore that such a refusal indicates a systematic bias and helps to perpetuate the myth that crime is committed by a class of patently malevolent persons, significantly different from the rest of us.

Conclusion

From this perspective, the gun control debate can be seen as merely one aspect of an overall difference in worldview that divides liberals and conservatives. This difference is likewise exhibited in disputes about a variety of other basic social problems, such as the proper distribution of wealth, opportunity, and liberty in society. But perhaps one of the most striking features of the confrontation relates not to the difference between the two parties, but rather to their apparent similarities.

In both cases, what appear to be incongruous positions are revealed as arising from ideological considerations. In the light of those considerations, it is clear that the apparent incongruities reflect a fundamental consistency. Moreover, it is these considerations that determine attitudes quite independently of the specifics of any particular issue in the area of crime control.

In relation to gun control, the heavy ideological cast to the debate means that minds are made up very early when specific proposals are being discussed. Indeed, what is specific in the proposals is frequently ignored altogether. Conclusions cannot be arrived at because they were already reached before discussion began.

This ideological cast has inhibited any collaboration between parties. There might be, in fact, much common ground on specific proposals between gun control opponents and the pro-gun control constituency that has developed in recent years. But perception of the common ground is obscured by a cloud of animosity generated by extrinsic doctrinal disputes.

Absorption with grand strategy precludes rational discussion at the tactical level.

So there is some value in recognizing the ideological roots underlying the gun control debate. Of course, insight into the ideological content of our own sentiments and ideas does not ensure that we shall be able to solve the problem, but understanding the ideological roots of our beliefs can increase the likelihood of our becoming aware of unexamined premises. At the same time, it can make us sensitive to unconsidered possibilities of compromise and collaboration.

REFERENCES

Hoover, John Edgar. *Persons in Hiding*. Boston: Little, Brown, 1938.

Sutherland, Edwin H., and Donald R. Cressey. *Principles of Criminology*, 9th ed. Philadelphia: Lippincott, 1974.

Van den Haag, Ernest. *Punishing Criminals*. New York: Basic Books, 1975.

Wilson, James Q. *Thinking About Crime*. New York: Vintage Books, 1977.

Zimring, Franklin E., and Gordon Hawkins. "Ideology and Euphoria in Crime Control," *University of Toledo Law Review* 10 (1979):370–388.

18

The Future of Federal Gun Laws: Two Scenarios

W hat types of public policy toward handgun ownership and use are likely in the United States three decades in the future? None of our acquaintances possesses a crystal ball sufficiently unclouded to provide clear answers to such questions, yet using the long-range future as a frame of reference can impose a useful discipline on current debates about firearms control.

In the first place, thinking about the future requires a more sustained analysis of historical trends than one usually encounters in contemporary discussion of firearms control in the United States. Quite simply, addressing the issue of where we are going over the course of the next few decades suggests an examination of where we have come from of at least equal length.

The second advantage of "futuristic" examination of handgun policy is that it requires the analyst to coordinate projections of public policy toward handguns with other social, technical, structural, and governmental trends that will shape the United States thirty years from now. A projected handgun policy must either fit with other anticipated future developments or create a form of intellectual friction in which handgun policy elements or other anticipated future conditions must be reexamined.

This chapter sketches two alternative national handgun futures. The first, "historically" derived, is a complex amalgam of federal, state, and local regulations characterized by federal minimum standards of accountability and eligibility of purchase, and also by wide variation among states and localities in imposing supplemental restrictions on possession and sale of handguns. The second, designed to "fit" with other anticipated future developments, projects much more restrictive federal control on eligibility for handgun ownership.

The first section discusses the major elements of the historically derived national handgun policy. The second section sketches a more restrictive federal handgun policy implemented as a response to anticipated social conditions thirty years from now. The third section discusses a few of the more important midterm trends that will determine which of these alternative futures will emerge.

Continuing Present Trends

If history is an appropriate guide, the next thirty years will bring a national handgun strategy composed of three parts:

(1) federally mandated or administered restrictions on handgun transfers that amount to permissive licensing and registration; (2) wide variation in state and municipal handgun possession and transfer regulation, with an increasing number of municipal governments adopting restrictive licensing schemes or "bans" on handgun ownership; and (3) increasing federal law enforcement assistance to states, and more particularly, to cities attempting to enforce more restrictive regimes than the federal minimum. Under such a scheme, federal law will neither set quotas on the number of handguns introduced into civilian markets nor dictate ownership policy to the states. Rather, designated high-risk groups, such as minors, convicted felons, and former mental patients, will be excluded from ownership, as is presently the case.

The two major changes in federal law we anticipate are, first, a registration scheme that will link individual handguns to first owners in a central data bank and will require prior notification before handguns are transferred; and second: a federal law prohibiting firearms transfers when the possession of a handgun by the transferee would violate the laws of the municipality in which he resides—currently federal protection of this kind is available only if a state law would be violated. Centrally stored ownership data would permit federal law to extend to transfers made by nondealers, and regulations requiring timely prior notice of private transfers through dealers or local officials would be added to existing regulations.

The changes in federal law outlined in the preceding paragraphs would facilitate minimal municipal standards for residents acquiring handguns that could not be frustrated by more lenient state government standards. This new power, and a climate favorable to handgun regulation in the big cities, would produce a much larger list of metropolitan or city governments attempting to impose restrictive licensing or bans on civilian ownership among their populations. Presently existing systems in cities such as New York, Boston, Philadelphia, and Washington, D.C., would be emulated in cities such as San Francisco, Los Angeles, Chicago, and Detroit and in many other nonsouthern metropolitan areas. Within the South, municipal or metropolitan governments in areas like Miami and Atlanta might follow suit.

All of this would in turn increase the demand, particularly on the part of cities, for federal law enforcement support to protect city boundaries from in-state guns. Within five years after extension of federal protection to municipal handgun control, the intrastate, rather than interstate, migration of handguns will emerge as a major priority in federal firearms law enforcement.

It is, of course, one thing to make up a scheme of handgun regulation and quite another to argue that it is historically derived. Why is it that federal regulation will expand? What is the basis for suggesting that municipal handgun controls will increase? The answers to such questions are neither easy nor obvious.

National handgun registration is only peculiar in that it has not yet been accomplished. Since 1938, federal law has required most of the essential data for registration, but the records have been decentralized in a way that has effectively guaranteed they cannot be used. Two trends suggest momentum in the coming decades toward effectively centralized weapon ownership information. First, the development of efficient and cheap information processing removes any technical barrier to a national handgun data bank. Whatever the circumstances of 1938, we now face a situation where the marginal cost of creating an accountability system for handguns is minimal and the establishment of central data files would be neither technically difficult nor excessively costly.

The ease and cheapness with which weapons can be first-owner registered suggest a shift in the debate about registration from cost factors to more basic principles. Public opinion seems solidly behind handgun-owner accountability if registration is viewed solely as an accountability system and not as a first step toward confiscation of all the guns linked to registered owners. Registration thus seems inevitable if its proponents can make a creditable case that a registration scheme will not be used to facilitate a shift from permissive to restrictive licensing policies. This could be achieved by "grandfathering" all guns registered to eligible owners, so that any subsequent shift in federal regulatory policy would exempt validly registered guns.

The momentum toward tighter municipal licensing is easier to demonstrate. In the cities, pressure for handgun restriction has increased dramatically in the past fifteen years, and those cities that have adopted controls almost never repeal them. The momentum toward further handgun restriction in major metropolitan areas appears substantial in all regions except the South and the Southwest.

However, federal handgun registration and more restrictive municipal handgun control are by no means inevitable. Each initiative carries within it the seeds of its own defeat. In the case of registration, the principal potential villain is public and gun owner perception that accountability measures are merely one further step toward prohibition. The effort to secure prohibition in the name of registration has an old federal pedigree, dating from the National Firearms Act of 1934 and its successful attempt to deal with machine guns. Gun owner perception that registration means confiscation is widespread. Whether such perceptions can ward off a general trend toward centralization of automatic data processing is questionable.

The momentum toward further municipal handgun control seems unstoppable, but this too may be misleading. The key issue here is whether sustained attempts at municipal restriction are viewed as successful. In large part, municipal efforts to create handgun scarcity have not been conspicuously successful. Very few cities have experienced either the costs or benefits of tight controls. All this may end as we accumulate long-term experience with the new Washington, D.C., statute and with those cities that will follow in its wake.

Substantial changes in municipal and state regulation of handgun ownership have become the rule rather than the exception in those American jurisdictions that have reconsidered handgun regulation in the last twenty years. This has occurred despite complaints about the power of the gun control lobby.

The trend, viewed historically, is toward a patchwork quilt of federal, state, and local regulation. This is not surprising. Significant variations exist in attitudes toward handguns, and it is only to be expected that these attitudinal differences should more quickly lead to a wider spectrum of state and local variation than to a unified national strategy. But will such incremental and differential policies produce adequate public protection three decades hence?

Handgun Scarcity as Federal Policy

The principal difficulty associated with the evolution of a national handgun policy based on state and local variation is that it might not work. Federal attempts to protect tight control in cities and states would continue to be frustrated by interstate and intrastate movement of handguns; the large civilian inventory of handguns would make efforts at accountability based on registration data both expensive and easy to frustrate.

Under such circumstances, greater concern with violent crime and reforms that spread the risk of violent crime more evenly across metropolitan areas, may produce a climate in which more stringent handgun controls may be demanded. Unless the increased fear associated with interdependence is offset by lower rates of violence, it is unlikely that increased public police expenditure or further increases in imprisonment rates alone will lead to tolerable levels of citizen risk. Progress toward a "cashless society" may reduce the incentive for personal robbery and may redistribute the risk of commercial robbery from cashless to cash-holding institutions, but the coincidence of interdependent urban life and freely available handguns will put pressure on "evolutionary" federal handgun policy.

An alternative federal handgun policy would stress substantially reducing the population of handguns and thus reducing general handgun availability. Federal standards would require the states to administer handgun-licensing systems that would deny most citizens the opportunity to possess handguns and handgun ammunition. The central features of this scheme are the commitment of federal policy to nationwide handgun scarcity, a policy that would be imposed on many states and cities where more permissive approaches were preferred, and a policy shift making possession of handguns by million of households unlawful. Further, whatever the division of responsibility among federal, state, and local law enforcement, this approach would, unlike others, put the federal government in the standard-setting—and, most likely, production control—business.

What one calls such regulation is a secondary matter. Federal "restrictive licensing" is the equivalent of a "national handgun ban." Indeed, many "ban" bills would leave more guns in circulation than would restrictive licensing because the exceptions—for example, security guards—are broad. The thrust of such a policy is the transition from a 35-million-handgun society to a 3-million-handgun society. This would be no small step.

Even if a national policy of handgun scarcity were wholeheartedly adopted, there are limits on the capacity of federal authorities to implement policy without state and local cooperation. Handgun production quotas and regulations governing the distribution of new weapons could be administered at the federal level. Determination of whether individual citizens who apply for licenses meet "need" criteria must be left to local officials, however, and removing unlawfully possessed handguns is a by-product of local police activity. The only way to shift this burden to the federal level is to create a national street police force, a radical departure from current practice that should neither be expected nor desired. Thus, even federal policies that attempt to centralize authority to reduce existing handgun ownership will operate at the mercy of state and local law enforcement.

Still, any such national standard setting would represent two major departures from present federal law. First, the federal government would attempt to limit the supply of handguns nationwide. Second, to reduce substantially the handgun population, citizens would be denied the opportunity to own weapons even if they were not part of special high-risk groups and in spite of less-restrictive policy preferences at the state and local level, where they reside.

This type of plenary federal policy has never been seriously considered in the United States. Early in the New Deal, Attorney General Homer Cummings proposed tight federal handgun controls that received scant congressional attention. In the 1970s a series of proposals to create federal restrictive licensing was introduced and soundly defeated. The urban experiments with restrictive licensing in New York City and Washington, D.C., both involved jurisdictions with small inventories of lawfully possessed handguns and cooperative local law enforcement.

If present trends continue, thirty years from now the majority of American citizens will still live in states with less-restrictive handgun policies than the proposed federal standard. Under what conditions, then, would this majority's congressional representatives vote for more stringent regulation than state legislatures would support? A restrictive national handgun policy would represent a turning point in public opinion and legislative climate, a relatively sharp departure from the previous twentieth-century politics of handgun control.

Midterm Policies and Long-Range Goals

The road to patchwork federalism in handgun policy requires different midterm regulatory approaches than if the long-term goal were civilian scarcity. Patchwork federalism can, of course, be achieved through the gradual accretion of actions by cities, states, and the federal government. To the extent that we follow this path, however, it might become increasingly difficult to make a later shift to a national scarcity policy.

There are three ways that state and city permissive controls could inhibit restrictive federal controls.

First, state and city regulations will have the effect of legitimizing handgun possession for those who obtain their guns legally in the city. Second, the inventory of handguns in circulation is likely to grow rapidly under patchwork federalism. Third, people who registered their guns under a federal registration plan would almost certainly be "grandfathered" when the shift to a national scarcity policy occurs. Each of these problems is discussed in more detail in the following pages.

THE IMPACT OF LOCAL REGISTRATION

Those states and cities that institute programs of owner registration create a population of handguns registered in good faith. One important consequence of registration is that it confers an explicit legal legitimacy on the continued ownership of a weapon by its owner. If a city adopts a registration scheme and later decides to create further restrictions on handguns, the more restrictive policy will usually exempt those owners with prior registration from additional eligibility requirements as long as they continue to possess their registered weapons.

The impact of this type of "grandfather clause" on the inventory of firearms or the availability of guns for misuse would vary from city to city. In a city with a small number of registered guns, such as New York or Washington, D.C., the effect of a grandfather clause on handgun availability would be small. But in major cities where the population of registered handguns is several hundreds of thousands, the inevitable result of the grandfather clause would be a large pool of guns at risk of theft or illegal transfer for many years after a shift to more restrictive ownership criteria. Most major cities have very large handgun inventories. Registration systems, if effective, would legitimate millions of handguns, and the handgun owner wishing to immunize himself from restrictions on continued ownership would be well advised to enter the system.

Grandfathering a large number of registered handguns might put pressure on the principle as well as on the practicality of municipal restrictive licensing. With so many prior registrants legally able to own weapons, it would be somewhat more difficult to argue that latecomers should be required to prove a special need for a gun before being eligible to acquire one. Further, the period during which a shift to more restrictive strategies was debated might create a large volume of handgun sales to new purchasers anticipating further restriction.

INVENTORY CONSEQUENCES OF CONTINUED FEDERALISM

In the twelve years after the Gun Control Act of 1968, more than 20 million handguns were added to the civilian handgun inventory in the United States. This total probably represents more than half the stock of operable handguns in the United States and a larger portion of the handguns involved in violent crime. Each year of federal indifference to handgun supply adds up to about 2 million pistols and revolvers to an inventory of weapons that a restrictive policy would seek to shrink. How much of an additional burden this imposes on future restrictive efforts cannot be estimated because we do not know how long new handguns remain operable and because it is not possible to estimate the impact of government repurchase efforts. But each year of unrestricted aggregate handgun supply makes the transition to national handgun scarcity more difficult and more expensive.

FEDERAL REGISTRATION AS A NATIONAL GRANDFATHER CLAUSE

Federal handgun registration would replicate the problems that state and local systems present for restrictive policies on a grand scale. At minimum, gun registration records could not be used as the basis for a recall of handguns once more restrictive policies were put in place. This limitation would almost certainly be inserted into the legislation that would initially enable central storage of handgun ownership information.

It is also likely that considerable pressure would be exerted to exempt registered handguns from whatever new ownership restrictions might subsequently be imposed, as long as the guns remained in possession of the registrant. This would make the move toward tight eligibility prospective in its effect and gradual in its impact on handgun inventory. How much delay this type of provision would produce is not known because there are no good data on how long handguns are retained in particular households.

"Specter Effects" of Restrictive Control Proposals

Public discussion of handgun restrictions or bans has an important influence on all aspects of the debate over firearms control. As previously mentioned, permissive licensing and registration are frequently opposed because they are regarded as "first steps" toward more restrictive policies. Restrictive proposals for handguns are feared as a step toward restriction on long gun ownership.

Fear about future restriction might play a role in the high level of demand for weapons available now and possibly not available in the future. Further, there is evidence that opposition to restrictive control has increased as the issue has received public attention. From the standpoint of an advocate firmly committed to permissive licensing and registration as ultimate federal law, the policy climate might have been better if proposals for restrictive handgun policies had not surfaced in the late 1960s.

What are the prospects now for shelving the debate about handgun restriction in favor of a permanent compromise at the federal level? Any such proposal would probably be regarded as inauthentic, and doubts about the effectiveness of federal neutrality on handgun ownership policy suggest that any "permanent compromise" of that sort would fail to satisfy those who regard handgun violence as a serious national problem. The issue of national handgun policy is thus unlikely to be resolved with a long-standing compromise despite the manifold impact of restrictive federal handgun proposals.

Conclusion

In the long run, changing public attitudes about guns and gun legislation will determine the course of federal handgun policy. Accordingly, the next chapter examines what kinds of attitude changes are likely to influence the federal legislative picture and what early indicators of opinion change observers might look for.

REFERENCES

Jones, Edward D. III. "The District of Columbia's 'Firearms Control Regulations Act of 1975': The Toughest Handgun Control Law in the United States—Or Is It?" *Annals of the American Academy of Political and Social Sciences* 455 (1981):138–149.

Leff, Carol Skalnick, and Mark H. Leff. "The Politics of Ineffectiveness: Federal Firearms Legislation 1919–38," *Annals of the American Academy of Political and Social Sciences* 455 (1981):48–62.

Moore, Mark H. "Keeping Handguns from Criminal Offenders," *Annals of the American Academy of Political and Social Sciences* 455 (1981):92–109.

Smith, Tom W. "The 75% Solution: An Analysis of the Structure of Attitudes on Gun Control, 1959–1977," *Journal of Criminal Law and Criminology* 71 (1980):300–316.

Zimring, Franklin E. "Firearms and Federal Law: The Gun Control Act of 1968," *Journal of Legal Studies* 4 (1975):133–192.

19

Social Change, Public Attitudes, and the Future of Handgun Control

Many factors can influence the direction of future handgun policy. A sharp decline in public fear of crime would decrease demand for handguns; at the same time, if this resulted in reduced violent crime, it would reduce the need for handgun control. An increase in burglary rates or, more significantly, in rates of home-invasion robbery would work the other way.

However, the most important element of future policy is not the crime rates but social notions of appropriate crime countermeasures. The social status of the household self-defense handgun in our cities and suburbs will emerge as a critical leading indicator of future federal handgun control. Public opinion research has indicated that self-defense in the home is the most important "good reason" given for handgun ownership. If citizens continue to believe that possessing a loaded handgun is a respectable method of defending urban households, handgun demand and opposition to restrictive policy will continue.

If owning loaded handguns in the home comes to be viewed more as part of the gun problem than as a respectable practice, the prospects for restrictive control will improve over time. The residual uses of handguns—informal target shooting, collection, and hunting sidearms—are peripheral to the handgun control controversy. Household self-defense is a central issue.

Public attitudes toward handguns for self-defense are related to fear of crime, but there are other factors that bear on the respectability of the urban housegun. One is alternative self-defense measures, such as burglar alarms, silent alarms that trigger police or private security responses, and the house dog. Most of these measures are more effective at preventing burglary than handguns, but are less effective against personal injuries once the home invader is inside.

A second influence on attitudes toward handguns in the home is public perception of the costs of weapon ownership within the household and in the wider community. Household accidents and guns recycled from homes to street crime are two kinds of loss that may influence public opinion about loaded guns in the home. Gun homicide involving family members may also influence the attitude of non–gun-owners, but it is likely that most gun-owning families would believe this kind of loss "can never happen to us."

An increase in the social stigma associated with household defense guns will influence the demand for handguns long before it affects national policy toward handgun supply. In the midterm, increasing stigma should reduce the proportion of households purchasing guns and increase the households that report considering and rejecting a handgun purchase. These indications should first appear in younger age segments of the population rather than households with older heads and established patterns of handgun ownership.

Upper middle class families "resettling" in older city neighborhoods might be a particularly interesting group to watch. These families have the economic resources to pursue alternative methods of household security. This segment of the population is well known for its trendsetting influence in other areas of style and consumption.

The early indications of a turning point in attitudes toward handguns will be more a function of attitude than hard data trends in crime rates or aggregate gun ownership. This is, in one sense, appropriate because the distinctive feature of the growth in handguns for self-defense has been more a question of perceived need than statistical risk. Handgun ownership reported in public opinion polls is higher among high-income groups than among low-income groups and as great in small cities as in big cities. But violent crime risks are greater for low-income groups and in larger cities. While the polls show white household ownership in excess of black household ownership, the risk of violent crime victimization is greater among black city residents.

Whatever happens will probably happen gradually. Thus, the condition for what might be viewed as a revolutionary shift in public policy is an evolutionary change in public attitude. As is so often the case, any discussion of this kind of shift as a future development must acknowledge that this type of attitude change may already be in progress. Early indications of how the debate on handguns will be resolved may be found in the action and beliefs of key opinion leadership groups in the next ten or fifteen years. A short list of such opinion leaders includes women, blacks, the elderly, and the young.

Women

Rapid change in the status of women is one of the most important social changes associated with America's recent past and near future. At the same time, women have played a remarkable dual role in public opinion about handguns. Female ownership of self-defense handguns has historically been low, but female vulnerability to violent crime has been one of the most persuasive reasons offered as a justification for household handguns. President Reagan was not alone when he justified a gun in the dresser drawer as particularly suited for periods when he would be away from the ranch. Generations of men, who are not themselves supposed to be afraid in their own households, have kept handguns "for the little woman."

Two things are striking about women's dual role. First, both low ownership and the woman's role as justification for the gun are based on traditional sex roles and patterns of family organization. Second, it is inevitable that either female handgun ownership patterns or "the little woman" as an excuse for household self-defense guns will have to change in the near future.

The reason for this is simple demographics. In the 1960s, when 7 percent of the people who bought handguns were women, fewer than a fifth of all American households were headed by females. Since the mid-1960s, the growth in female-headed households has been enormous, and the majority of these are women living alone. Since 1969, the number of households without adult men has gone from under 13 million to over 20 million and from under a fifth to over a quarter of all households. Either these women will acquire weapons at historically unprecedented rates or they will blow the cover on female vulnerability as a justification of gun ownership.

The American woman of the late 1980s and 1990s will thus be the first and most important leading indicator of the social status of self-defense handguns in the more distant future. If female ownership of self-defense handguns increases dramatically, the climate of opinion for drastic restriction of handguns will not come about. Women are physically more vulnerable to crime than men, and this special vulnerability, other liberations aside, will be an important part of our culture for generations. Women, predominantly, are targets of sexual violence.

Further, female attitudes toward household burglary, far and away the most frequent form of home victimization, seem to diverge from male attitudes. Many men tend to shrug off burglary as a loss of property; women experience it as a gross invasion of personal privacy that produces high levels of fear and insult. If single women demand guns for self-defense purposes, federal firearms control will, at maximum, require screening, waiting periods, and some registration. The 50-million-handgun society of the future may be foreordained.

But what if a substantial majority of America's single women reject the handgun as a personal option? There are other antiburglary options: dogs, alarm systems, deadbolt locks. And there are indications that women feel differently about gun ownership. One Harris poll showed that total gun ownership in female-headed households was less than half that reported by households including an adult male.

The political and cultural implications of persistently low handgun ownership by single women are also potentially enormous: A large and growing segment of the electorate will not own handguns. And the special vulnerability of this group makes them immune to arguments that other groups really need handguns or that they are being insensitive to the fear of crime.

As important might be the impact of single women's behavior on the sexual politics of handgun ownership within marriage. Women, particularly mothers, do not like to have lethal weapons in their homes. How does Mr. Smith convince Mrs. Smith that a gun is necessary for her "when he is away" if some of her best friends live alone without guns? This is the kind of moral ammunition wives may put to effective use as they become more confident of their capacity to participate in such decisions as equal partners.

Continued low handgun ownership by women is not a sufficient condition to stigmatize handgun ownership, but it will be necessary to any emerging long-range consensus. Already, antihandgun meetings seem to be composed in unequal proportion of emphatic wives and reluctant husbands. Perhaps, in searching for the eventual solution to the American handgun stalemate, we should redirect our attention from the *New York Times* to *Ms.* magazine and the *Ladies' Home Journal*.

Blacks

White America lives in fear of violence in a rather abstract way. An astonishingly high proportion of black Americans have tasted violence firsthand in the lives of their families and close friends. The enormous difference in levels of violent crime victimization between urban minorities and the rest of the country makes the issue of the self-defense handgun far more urgent for urban blacks and gives the black community special credentials for teaching the costs and benefits of the handgun.

To date, blacks—absorbed by other pressing problems— have not played a role in the heated debate over handgun control. Indeed, one of the most striking characteristics of both pro- and antihandgun lobbies is their lily-white leadership. This will change. A large and growing black middle class, imprisoned by residential segregation, lives next door to the urban American ghetto and in constant fear. For the black urban family, there is often no middle ground: Handguns are either purchased or detested.

Many black women, mothers of sons, are involuntary experts on handguns in the house and on the streets. Their men and male children, living high-risk lives, have better reasons to buy guns than any other segment of American society and better reasons not to buy guns. Handguns loom as a major source of friction between the sexes, between the classes, and between generations in many black communities.

The outcome of such conflicts is difficult to forecast. Decisive rejection of self-defense guns on the fringes of the American ghetto could be an important message to mainstream America. On the other hand, an increase in self-defense handgun ownership within the black middle class, and particularly among female-headed households, would represent a major obstacle to the political climate that might promote handgun scarcity.

The Elderly

The numbers and influence of what we often refer to as senior citizens have increased dramatically in the past two decades and will continue to increase. This segment of the population, politically active and well informed, lives in constant fear of crime in the city. The combination of substantial political clout and special vulnerability to crime has already produced special legislation stiffening the penalties for those who victimize the elderly. There is, to our knowledge, no consensus among Americans over sixty-five on the issue of handgun restriction. But this group, predominantly female, is another source of potential leadership in building social consensus about the loaded household handgun.

In male-headed households, however, gun ownership patterns may tend to persist. Because the loaded handgun in the urban home is a relatively new phenomenon, the coming years will witness the first large generation of urban handgun ownership becoming older. The mix of factors that might change ownership and attitudes in an aging population is substantial: an increase in the proportion of female-headed households, increasing fear of crime, perhaps a decrease among older men in the need for machismo artifacts, and a general shift in life situations from offensive orientations toward crime to more defensive adaptations.

Whether all this leads to consensus is anybody's guess. Probably not. However, the potential impact of a unified senior citizen's lobby is substantial. For those who view the power of the National Rifle Association as awesome in legislative circles, imagine what would happen if that organization had opposed the last round of Social Security increases. The critical questions, therefore, are whether older America can come close to consensus on the handgun issue and what that consensus will be.

The Young

Habits are easier to avoid than to break. It is probably much easier to talk a young person out of acquiring his first home self-defense handgun than to persuade his father that the household appliance he has retained, loaded, and kept ready for twenty years is of no use to his family. If this is the case, the emerging generation of late adolescents and young adults is a leading indicator here as in so many other areas of manners, morals, and behavior.

The first leading indicator of the future of the urban house gun might be the behavior of the young upper middle class in major urban areas. But antihandgun sentiments must trickle down to middle and working class young America and into its suburbs before the elements of political consensus fall into place. It is here that the opinion leadership of women, mentioned above, must play a critical role.

Conclusion

A realistic view of the future provides hope only for optimists among antihandgun groups but small comfort as well for the friends of the urban American handgun. Only an agnostic is on safe ground. In the complexities and pace of American social change, there is a potential coalition of opinion that could lead to change in public attitude and public law regarding handgun ownership. But potential, of course, is the word we hear most often from coaches of losing teams, and the bitter rhetoric and inflated claims associated with some current antigun propaganda and legislation may retard the evolution toward a constructive consensus.

Opinion-leading groups may identify the boundaries of American handgun politics in the next generation far more quickly than they or we suspect. In making this assertion, we do not mean to understate the role of spectacular tragedies in prompting political action on guns. The Martin Luther King, Jr., and Robert Kennedy killings were absolutely necessary to the passage of the federal gun laws in 1968. The murder of John Lennon and shooting of President Reagan had a powerful impact on public opinion. No doubt, some future gun tragedy might provide the spur for further legislation, but these episodes explain more about when we pass laws than how far our gun laws can be pushed as an instrument of social change.

REFERENCES

Bruce-Biggs, B. "The Great American Gun War," *The Public Interest* 45 (1976):37–62.

Zimring, Franklin E. "Violence and Firearms Policy." In Lynn A. Curtis, ed., *American Violence and Public Policy*. New Haven, Conn.: Yale University Press, 1985.

CHAPTER

20

Short-Term Costs, Long-Term Benefits

The subject of this chapter can be distinguished from our earlier discussion of the costs of gun control in Chapter 16 because here we view the subject of costs in a broader perspective and consider also the possible benefits that regimes of firearms control might produce. Our analysis here may also be contrasted with the discussion in Chapter 19, because there we attempted to identify some of the determinants of public attitude and social change, whereas here we speak normatively

193

of the values that *should* determine attitudes to gun control. More specifically, we discuss here the considerations that we find persuasive in reaching our own view of the wisdom of attempting to restrict access to handguns in America.

Neither of us is by profession a futurist, if indeed that is a profession. But we have noticed, among those who do speak and write about the future, a striking contrast in attitude depending on whether it is the near-term or long-term future of gun control that is being considered. As to the near-term, it was conventional wisdom long before the Reagan presidency that the passage of restrictive national legislation was all but impossible. Through all of the four presidential administrations succeeding that of Lyndon Johnson the idea of a national policy of strict handgun control was considered a millennial dream rather than a proximate legislative possibility. And this opinion was jointly held by supporters and opponents of gun control.

As a more remote prospect, however, handgun scarcity has been seen as both desirable and achievable by those who speculate about the role of firearms in American society in the future. Many who doubt the possibility of the implementation of controls over handguns in the present, or in the immediate future, regard the ultimate achievement of the restriction of easy access to such weapons as not merely possible but probable. This kind of conflict between short-term and long-term prognostications is of course not confined to the gun control controversy. Those acquainted with the death penalty debate will recognize a familiar attitudinal pattern.

There are also contrasts between short-term and the long-term calculations that are of critical significance in evaluating the feasibility of implementing a policy of severe restriction on gun ownership. No restrictive firearms policy can pay for itself in the short run. The dissensions and discontinuities and the start-up costs in resources and energy inevitably associated with attempts to bring about major changes in gun ownership patterns and in weapon availability will be considerable. And such costs will tend to be at their heaviest in the early years of a new policy. By contrast, the most significant benefits that will accrue from such initiatives will not be immediate, but rather incremental and cumulative as the available supply of weapons diminishes.

The most marked reduction in firearms violence cannot be expected until well past the introduction of legislation designed to achieve handgun scarcity and long after the period of most intense social and political detriment or cost. Gun control is thus best seen as a social capital investment program the perceived desirability of which depends on the acceptance of a strongly future oriented public policy.

There are those for whom the decision to make the substantial investment required at the front end for a genuine attempt to restrict the availability of handguns will be relatively easy to make. Those who regard the achievement of handgun scarcity as not merely desirable but historically inevitable are unlikely to be daunted by the prospect of heavy transitional costs. If these costs must be paid, the fact of heavy initial cost is not a major deterrent.

In fact, the real social and monetary costs of introducing restrictive handgun control in 1965 would probably have been less than half the costs of introducing the same program today because the number of handguns in circulation has so sharply escalated. And this acceleration and the extension of gun ownership in our time is the most powerful argument for substantial social investment in gun control before matters get too much worse.

For those who do not regard widespread handgun availability as incompatible with modern urban life, the high ratio of costs to benefits in the short term does provide a cogent argument against the introduction of controls. Thus, one crucial question about the advisability of taking decisions now about legislating for handgun scarcity turns on the acceptability of the prospect of 50 million handguns in circulation half or three-quarters of a century hence in the United States.

If the United States can indefinitely tolerate tens of millions of handguns, the burden of proof, in relation to the desirability of introducing stringent controls soon, rests firmly on the proponents of change. But once the reduction of the general availability of handguns is seen as an inevitable feature of the maturation of American urban culture, it is hard to see what argument can be made against taking immediate steps toward that goal.

Many years ago Maynard Keynes, writing about paying short-run costs for long-run benefits, observed ironically that in the long run we are all dead. In this case, however, failure to pay short-run costs will mean that for many American citizens there will be no long run.

Index

Index